BOOKS BY NORMAN VINCENT PEALE

YOU CAN WIN
THE ART OF LIVING

YOU CAN WIN

NORMAN VINCENT PEALE

THE ABINGDON PRESS

NEW YORK   CINCINNATI   CHICAGO

PEALE
YOU CAN WIN

Copyright, 1938, by
NORMAN VINCENT PEALE

Printed in the United States of America

First Edition Printed November, 1938
Second Printing, November, 1938

TO MY WIFE
RUTH STAFFORD PEALE

CONTENTS

PREFACE

LIFE has a key, and to find that key is to be assured of success in the business of living. Surely some usable implement exists which can make life work. We are all faced with certain practical considerations—how to get enough money to pay the bills, how to get along with people, how to meet discouragement, failure, illness, and sorrow. Problems clamor about our distracted minds—love, marriage, children, the home. There are matters of physical health, nerve strength, emotional stability. One's work, his business or job, his future development and attainments—all add to that intricate and confused phenomenon called a man's life. Some people never succeed in straightening it out. They muddle through after a fashion and perhaps manage to be fairly happy and passingly successful. Others do not even muddle through.

But why muddle—why fail in the problem of living? Life is a puzzle, to be sure, frequently even a fearful tangle, but to every puzzle there is an answer, to every tangle there is a solution. Anything that has so much evidence of intelligence in its creation as the natural world and human life must have a correspondingly intelligent method of successful operation. If a savage of common intelligence should come upon a complicated mechanism like an airplane with no one to explain it, he would, of course, be bewildered by the questions it would raise. There would be two natural assumptions, however—first, that so perfect an assembly required intelligence and purpose, and, second, that though it eluded him, some way of operating the machine did exist. The parable is obvious. We come

9

upon this bewildering creation described under the general term "life," meaning the world and ourselves and others and God and all that goes to make up our conscious and unconscious experience. May we not also reasonably assume that there is a technique for working it successfully, a method for making it go?

The author believes he knows of a way to make life work. He has tested it in his own experience and has found that it works for him when worked. He has enjoyed the opportunity of observing its application in the lives of a vast number of people who have likewise found that it works. The author firmly holds to the conviction that any individual who will apply the method of living and attitude of mind outlined in this book will have an amazing and never-failing secret by which he can gloriously win on that battlefield called Life.

Appreciative acknowledgment is made to the New York *Journal and American* and associated newspapers for permission to use certain material written by the author for their columns, and rearranged for this volume.

NORMAN VINCENT PEALE.

New York City.

CHAPTER I

WHY I KNOW YOU CAN WIN

NO man is defeated until he thinks he is. The world may lay waste his land and break through his outer fortifications, but as long as the inner citadel of his life remains untaken he can win the battle. A wise old Book tells us that the issues of life are out of the heart. Of a truth they are, and if a man's heart is sturdy, what can the world do to him? Its only recourse in the presence of indomitable courage and faith is to capitulate. The world inevitably gives in to the man who won't give up. Adversity comes in varying form to all men, but some men have the ability to turn misfortune to advantage. James Russell Lowell wisely said, "Mishaps are like knives that either serve us or cut us as we grasp them by the blade or the handle." The secret of winning in life is to get a firm hold on the handle.

One's reaction to mishap and difficulty is determined by the sort of spirit one has within him. Your world, the world you live in day by day, is just about what you make it. It will be no better or bigger or finer than you are yourself.

The inner braces of a man's heart must be equal to the outer pressure of life's circumstances. Let the outer pressure be increased, or even continuously sustained, and the inner support weakened, and life falls in. Long ago I came across a sentence from Thomas Carlyle upon which, the more I see of life, I have had reason to ponder. And the sentence is this: "It was always a serious thing to live." It was never an easy thing,

11

certainly not for any extended length of time, to meet
and survive the various hazards of human experience.
To stand up against the bullying process of nature is
serious business. To meet and triumph over disappointment, adversity, sorrow, and failure is not easy.
To avoid or overcome the hostility and misunderstanding of individuals or groups of individuals is difficult.
Carlyle was right—"It was always a serious thing to
live"—and little wonder he also declared that the chief
question life asks of each of us is—"Wilt thou be a hero
or a coward?"

Hugh Walpole, in one of his novels, echoes the same
thought. One of his characters is made to say a great
thing: "It isn't life that matters; it's the courage you
bring to it." It is a certainty that the soft and pam-
pered personality will not get very far with the problem
of victorious living. If one's spirit is heroic and has a
drawing account on the bank of inner power and re-
source, he will win out in the end.

You may this very day be face to face with critical
problems, or you may be bearing heavy burdens and
responsibilities, and perhaps you are a bit discouraged,
if not quite overwhelmed. It is possible that you are
even tempted to give up. We all know how you feel,
for there isn't one of us who has not felt just like that
a good many times. But you are not going to be defeated. Press deeper into your spirit and there you will
find an indomitable, glorious conqueror nothing in this
world can overcome.

There are several selves, or personalities, in each of
us, and one of them is a timid, little self that meets life
with fear and trembling. I notice a cartoon in the
paper about a man named Milquetoast, or The Timid
Soul. That is in all of us to some extent. This timid

self prevents us sometimes from attaining our cherished ambitions.

I read of a woman in one of those small apartments in New York City where the bed comes out of the wall and you pull the kitchen sink out of a drawer when you want to prepare a meal. This woman had a dog, a little snip of a thing, that as far as size was concerned was about right for the little apartment. The trouble was, however, that he had a bark much too large for so small a space, so she went to a doctor and had him operated on, with the result that his bark was reduced about eighty-five per cent. Many of us have done the same thing. We have allowed the stern difficulties of life to frighten us so that our timid little self has had its bark reduced. Accordingly, we make a feeble and futile impression upon life. Remember, you are a rugged soul, and that you have it in you to seize fate by the throat and dictate your own terms to it.

It is folly, of course, to expect to achieve such a victory on the basis of your own strength. No man, however resourceful or pugnacious, is a match for so great an adversary as a hostile world. He is at best a puny and impotent creature quite at the mercy of the cosmic and social forces in the midst of which he dwells. His only hope is to attach himself to some force superior to and more powerful than the world of things. Obviously the material world provides no force of this character, for all of its forces, such as wealth or fame or power over one's fellows, are themselves weak and ineffectual in the presence of fate and circumstance. People with great wealth and favored position, who exercise influential power, are quite as subject to the troubles and woes of life as their less fortunate neighbors. You cannot win over life by mere possession of money or position. Many who have attained these objectives are still the unhappy victims of fear and anxiety, harassed by feelings of inadequacy and constantly in fear of being unequal to the demands put upon them. They are haunted by the specter of a possible failure. Having put their faith in material things, they are obsessed with the possible tragedy of losing these values. Nor do their possessions relieve them from the fact that they have sensitive human personalities in which inner conflict works its havoc. In my interview work I find on the whole more personality disorganization among the favored class than among the common run of folk. It may be that greater leisure allows more time to think about oneself. It may be that heavier responsibility in the case of those who have positions of leadership breaks down nerve resistance. It may be that participation in the loose and pagan morality of our time is more general in this group. In privileged and unprivileged alike the repeated offenses against conscience and self-respect indulged in so freely today are producing, on the basis of what I see in my conference room, an abundant crop of obsessions and personality disarrangements.

The deeper we proceed in an analysis of the devices commonly supposed to open a way of victory over this hard world in which we live—devices such as wealth, power, sensory pleasure—the more certain it is that these are in themselves dead ends. We must relearn a truth our generation has forgotten but which all wise men know—that the center of power is within the spirit of man. Herodotus said, "The destiny of man is in his own soul." To win over the world a man must get hold of some power in his inward or spiritual life which will never let him down. Material things fail; riches tarnish; sensory responses become satiated and jaded; ambitions decay into disillusionment, but inner spiritual power constantly renews itself from deep springs of unlimited supply. Life never loses its flavor or fine taste. The spirit never grows weak or stale. One finds himself becoming more and more imperturbable, more conscious of power, more aware of an astounding invincibility in his soul. I am not overstating the matter. This confidence is based on the actual experience of countless people who have found there is a sure method by which they can win in life, come what may.

The secret of this inner power is the practice of real Christianity. I have never seen anything else that will give one complete victory over life. True, some people find a measure of power in art or music. I know a rich man with fading eyesight who seems to find strength to meet his affliction in a curious way. Late each night he goes alone into a chapel on his estate and plays the great pipe organ. As one hears the plaintive music coming from that darkened church, where a rich man going blind is seated at the organ seeking comfort for his soul, one is aware of the power of music to minister to the human spirit. Of course this power is itself spiritual, for, as Beethoven pointed out, "Music is more than a concord of sweet sounds; it is something from a higher world which we cannot describe, much less define, but which we have the power to invoke." The man in this story, it must be explained, has gained this admirable victory over his affliction from a deeper source than music. Like Abt Vogler, his temple of melody has afforded him a glimpse of the higher truth, that each of life's broken arcs ultimately becomes a perfect round. Thus one may tuck a sublime peace up against his soul, for he knows all will come out right in God's own time.

People who actually practice their Christian faith

find that it works in every situation. I referred to "real Christianity." By this phrase I mean to distinguish between that formal type of Christianity which works itself out in beliefs passively held, and that type where one puts his life with all of its concerns in the hands of God and, sincerely trying to live out Christ's spirit in daily life, trusts God to care for him, guiding him in his decisions and sustaining him by divine power and grace. The distinction has fine shadings, for even some faithful members of the church, living on a high moral and ethical standard, stop short of the Christianity I mean to define. They have a Christianity of beauty and character but there is beyond that a Christianity of spiritual power. In a mere ethical Christianity one struggles hard to "be good." In a Christianity of spiritual power one is given a superior strength whereby wrong impulses can no longer dominate him. In a formal Christianity one bears his burdens heavily and with a certain noble resignation. He still believes God can help to make the load lighter but never actually experiences that help. In a Christianity of spiritual power one gets a lifting power under his burdens far beyond anything his own strength can provide. It is as if a spiritual tide comes surging in with a vast shoulder as the ocean lifts a stranded vessel from mud flats.

I sat in a railroad train one morning which was filled with college students returning to school from their Christmas vacation. It was an interesting and animated scene, and a babel of conversation filled the car. Directly across the aisle was a group of girls who were greatly excited because at the next station one who was evidently very popular was expected to board the train. When that station was reached, the young lady for whom they waited came in with a rush and there was much feminine ado. But this was as nothing when they discovered on her finger a sparkling engagement ring. They plied her with questions which she tried to answer out of a rather attractive confusion, but finally she sought to silence them all by the sweeping declaration, "Oh, you'll never know what it means to be in love until you experience it." Little did those girls suspect that their conversation would be overheard and repeated in a book, but it is a perfect illustration of what I want to say. That young lady's statement is true about religion as well as love—"You'll never really know what it is until you experience it."

Broadly speaking, there are two types of Christianity. One is traditional or hereditary. Somebody once long ago experienced it. He found it for himself and handed it down to his descendants, many of whom, unfortunately, have treated it like an heirloom, to be preserved with honor, but from which the original freshness has long since departed. A couple came to our church at the heart of New York City one day to be married. They were accompanied by the parents of the groom, who proudly told me that they had been married in our church twenty-five years before, and the further interesting fact that the grandparents of one of them had been likewise married there over a half-century previously. I asked them where they were attending church at present and with a surprised laugh they said they did not go to church. They reminded me again, however, that the grandparents had been great servants of God and strong Christians. At home they still had the high silk hat which the grandfather had worn on his wedding day. They were, you see, preserving the grandfather's religion as they were preserving his hat. Both were heirlooms. Their religion was a tradition, not a present experience.

There is too much of this sort of religion in our

country. What was vital has now become a relic. It is a traditional religion. Our fathers were for the most part men of personal religious experience. Often was it said of them, "They had religion." That meant that God was real to them. Their hearts were warm with the impingement of the divine power upon their lives. They had an inner strength, a spiritual vitality and virility which made them strong and effective in their lives. They constituted a citizenship upon which this nation grew great and prospered. But they could not pass the experience on to their children, for obviously you cannot hand down an experience. It must be felt by each person anew and for himself. Religious experience cannot be bequeathed like stocks and bonds, and houses and lands. When you try to hand down an experience, the danger always is that it will lose its color and freshness and become ultimately a form infrequently observed, and even then without an adequate sense of its meaning. It is like an old and half-forgotten daguerreotype. The trouble today is that the spiritual life of the world is surfeited with a second-hand religion. It is possible and splendid that one generation should hand down the by-products of religion in the form of a fine culture and noble code of ethics, but religion will thin out, and with it culture and ethics, unless the spiritual impulse is freshly renewed from generation to generation. It is for this reason that periodically every two or three decades in American history a revival of pure religion has swept over the land, relighting the fires of personal and public devotion. Men have referred to these movements as periods of great awakening, and from each of them can be dated the renewal of America's spiritual, social, and even economic life. This is the transformation which takes place when hereditary and traditional religion gives way to religion as experience, new and powerful, in the life of the people. It is profoundly to be hoped that this will happen again in America, and that right soon. It alone can save us.

Thus, the second type of Christianity is religion as personal experience. If a re-emergence of religion as personal experience is the solution for the vitiated life of the nation, so will it restore the power of effective living to the individual. What do we mean by the term "religion as experience"? Briefly, it may be defined as the realization of God in one's own soul. It is not to get a new intellectual or credal conception of God, but to have your heart strangely warmed by a sense of his spiritual presence. After such an experience one does not wistfully listen to others tell what God means to them—he knows for himself. Something has happened to him. He has been changed by a power greater than himself. His life, like an electric bulb that was dark because it was not attached to the flow of electric power, has been firmly connected to the stream of God's grace which now flows through him. To use another figure and returning to the incident of the young ladies previously referred to, religion as experience is like falling in love. One may define love and describe it fervently, but one never completely understands or appreciates it until its mystic process has operated in his own experience.

Perhaps I may best illustrate my meaning by the incident of a young minister whom I know. He is a splendid fellow, cultured, able, and attractive in personality. His character is good in the finest and strongest sense of the word. He preached a religion of beautiful ethics and had a warm compassion for the poor and needy from an economic point of view. One day, however, he came under the influence of a great soul in whom he noticed a deeper experience. There was about this man a strange inner power, so that when he spoke, people's hearts became warm and wistful, and profound yearnings resulted in men and women made over. The young man became acutely aware of a lack in his life. He saw that he had been preaching only words and he said, "I will get this power or give up the ministry." He was in dead earnest, and with absolute sincerity he asked God to give him a new life. He surrendered himself wholly to God and, as always happens when a man honestly puts his life in God's hands, a new contact was established and the man's life became illumined by a mystic and ineffable light. The next Sunday the people filed into the church and leaned indolently back to hear the same old words. But the sermon had not proceeded for many minutes before they came forward on their seats, aware that something had happened. It was the same man outwardly there in the pulpit, but it became apparent they had a new minister. The word—the word made flesh—moved like fire in his speech, and as springtime passes with magic touch over a dead world so did the transforming power of God stir a congregation into new life and experience.

There is nothing like it. It is the one and only medicine that will cure a stale, sinful, or defeated life. This experience of religion will give a deep inner joy and gaiety of spirit. Life no longer will be satiated or without interest. It will be everlastingly fresh. Saint Paul told us about the unsearchable riches in Christ. That is how one will feel about life after the experience— he will have a new sense of peace and a deep quietness in the center of the soul. By means of it one will learn the secret of poise in the midst of the outer confusion of our time. His inner conflicts, being healed, the outer world will no longer overwhelm him. He will know that the outer world goes to pieces largely because one has gone to pieces on the inside. For the first time in his life one will know how to rest. Hitherto he has assumed that rest meant to give a change to the body and mind, but the new experience will teach him that the center of rest is in a soul at peace. He will see that true rest is expressed in the phrase, "O rest in the Lord." The inner restlessness at the center of his personality, the vague sense of guilt deep in the subconscious mind having been settled and solved, he can now find peace and rest that is beneficial and lasting. It is amazing what Christianity offers—power, peace, victory, deep, infectious happiness. What a pity that anyone should miss these blessings so freely offered! But no one need miss them. Put yourself completely in God's hands, and with Saint Paul you will be able to say, "The grace of our Lord flooded my life."

Thus your religion, which may now consist largely of the framework of belief, tradition and ceremonial, and from which you derive not a little comfort and help, can be—and this is the greatest truth you will ever encounter—a force and power to completely revolutionize your life. From it you can draw a power beyond anything you have ever experienced, a power sufficient to overcome any weakness, carry any burden, conquer any sin. Through a surrendered faith in Christ and a daily intimate living in spirit with him you can win over adversaries which formerly seemed too great for the human spirit to bear.

Call the roll of all those things which can defeat a man—suffering and pain, sorrow, disappointment, hardship, frustration, sin. There they stand, challenging, menacing, all but invincible. Who can hope to overcome them? But if one is armed with a strange and wonderful secret, these giants are at his mercy. This secret is not some cure-all, nicely wrapped in cellophane, which you can purchase in a store. It is

not an achievement for which you may valiantly
struggle. It cannot be purchased, nor can it be won by
effort. It is a gift freely offered to you. All you need
do is to take it by an act of faith and begin to live on it.
Why go on being a victim of fear, anxiety, trouble, and
weakness, with vigor of mind and spirit and body being
steadily drained off? Great new power and strength
can be yours.

Turn to the Bible. In the Bible you read a statement by a man who long ago discovered the truth. He
said, "I can do all things through Christ who giveth
me the strength." You can learn to say the same thing.
That secret can be yours if you want it. You can win.
I mean that because I know it is true. It is immaterial
what your difficulty is. If it is the worst difficulty in
the world, it does not invalidate the fact that you can
win if you will adopt this plan of living. There is
nothing magical about the Bible, but the secret I am
talking about is to be found within its pages. Why sit
there defeated when you have at your very elbow a
book that can make a new person of you? When you
open it, the most human people come walking out of its
pages and sit down with you or me and say: "Listen, I
have a secret and I want to share it with you. If you
take Christ into your life and put your life in his hands,
you too can win over anything." "I can do all things
through Christ," says the Bible.

I realize that many people do not understand religion in this vital way. They think of religion as something that has to do with what they regard as stale and
musty churches and dull services of worship. But
that isn't religion at all. Religion deals with an electric power or force which is all about us, just as sound
waves are in the air. When you come into your living
room, for instance, your radio is silent and lifeless.

You turn a dial. You tune your radio to the sound waves that are filling the air and immediately these sounds are brought into your room and you take into your consciousness that with which the air is filled but which the moment before were meaningless to you because you had not tuned in. All about us in the universe is this value called the power of God, but we are impervious to it. It means nothing to us. We are closed to it. We go on day by day living in our own feeble human strength, which is drawn from inside ourselves and which soon runs dry. Accordingly, we are worried; we are nervous; we are defeated time and time again; we have no sense of conquest at all. Religion means that you get tired of living like that. You become aware of a power in the world that you do not possess. What, then, do you do? You tune in. You bring your spirit into harmony with the Spirit of God. That's very simply done too. You say with the faith of a little child, "Lord, I bring my human spirit to you and I ask you to fill me with your power." Then the miracle happens. As the strains of an orchestra fill the room when a radio is tuned in, so the marvelous melody of God comes into your life. Then as you look at these things which formerly overwhelmed you, you can say with Saint Paul, "I too can do all things through Christ." Why am I so positive about all this? First, because I had the same experience myself. Anybody who wants to dispute the reality of this can do so to his heart's content but I know this is true because it happened to me, and the greatest argument in the world is to be able to say, "I have experienced it." The second reason I know it is true is because I have seen it happen frequently to other people.

But will this secret of real Christianity work in the actual life of a realistic world? The answer is that many people with problems identical to your own have discovered it will. Let us look at one or two areas of human experience to which the principle has been applied.

There, for example, is sorrow, a universal experience. In every home comes the day when a vacant chair speaks mutely of a dear one gone. Everywhere are people who long for "the touch of a vanished hand, and the sound of a voice that is still." Every man ultimately must face the problem of sorrow and the poignant longing for one he has loved long since and lost awhile. In my work as a clergyman I have been in countless homes of sorrow. I have stood by many a grave with bereaved families, beholding the sad obsequy wherein one dearly loved is lowered to a last resting place. Always the thought of the suffering of it profoundly impresses me. It is a cruel and terrific wrench of nature to take from a family circle one whose form and figure, whose smile and touch, the sound of whose voice is inexpressibly precious and to lay that one in the earth and go back to a cheerless place. Looking upon people in these circumstances I have often wondered how they bear it. It is surely one of the supreme crises of life and calls for resources more than human. If I believed in Christianity for no other reason, I should prize it for what I have seen it do for people in sorrow. If some mighty vandal should destroy our literature, two passages I would seek to save from the catastrophe would be these—"I am the resurrection and the life," and the other, "Let not your heart be troubled; ye believe in God, believe also in me—in my Father's house are many mansions." I would save them for the reason that I do not see how men and women could go on without them. From them I have seen the bereaved draw a mystic power that has sent them back from the place of heartbreak to the world of affairs with a strange light shining in their eyes. It is thrilling to see how a real Christian meets sorrow and to observe the working of the inner power under these most pathetic circumstances.

I had two funerals in one day. One in the morning of that day was in a very humble home, a place, clean and neat, but a home of poverty. Previously I had conducted funeral services there for two sons, and now the father was dead. Her family now all gone, the heartbroken wife and mother sat alone in her grief. She was clad in a simple, well-worn dress, long out of style. Her hands, lying clasped in her lap, were rough and red, the hands of a woman who had known only toil. Her head was bowed as I repeated to her the dear old words of comfort. She rocked slowly to and fro in her chair as I reminded her that in her faith she would find comfort and that God was near. Suddenly she looked up and her eyes were filled with tears, but there was a radiant light on her face like sunshine through summer rain. "Yes," she said softly, "I know—all that you say is true. I feel him; I feel him now. Christ has been here today. He is here now by my side."

A hush settled upon the room. The truth of her words could not be denied. I too felt a Presence. It seemed at any minute a third but unseen person would speak. Never in any cathedral has he been nearer than in that humble room. The simple little woman seemed to radiate spiritual power. Her face shone like a transfiguration and the conviction in her voice was electric, unworldly, as if she were face to face with God, as indeed she was. I saw in her, as in a flash, the ancient grandeur of the Christian faith. This simple woman marched up the steep ascent of heaven through peril, toil, and pain. Nothing could defeat her. In her I saw the indomitable, victorious spirit of a real Christian. She had something deep and true, a secret priceless beyond words. This was no time for histrionic display or pretty theories. Here was a woman up against about as stiff a proposition as one could imagine and I saw her win her battle. And the secret— Christ was with her. She had put her life in his hands and he did not fail her. Into her spirit he poured that ineffable value we call the grace of God, by which she became more than a conqueror. You see, it works in real life.

On the afternoon of the same day I sat with a leading business man of that city in his beautiful home. His wife was dead and he too sat in his grief. What a contrast with the other home of the morning! Here was all that wealth could provide of beauty and loveliness. Costly rugs were on the floor; exquisite pictures and hangings were on the walls. But what did it all matter?—a beloved wife was gone and a man whom I knew to be a strong leader in the business world was broken with grief.

Again I spoke the great old words, and he listened as a man thirsty for the water of life. I shall never forget what he told me in the tender friendship of that hour of sorrow. He was a man of somewhat austere mien, with no outward evidence of sentiment in his nature. He was a typical aggressive and efficient business man of the sort that compels respect and gains dominance. Within his home, however, he was dependent, leaning upon his wife, who was almost a mother to him. He was shy about social contacts and much preferred to remain at night quietly in his home reading, his wife knitting or reading on the opposite side of the table. As many men of similar type, he was a boy never quite grown up but putting on a strong front before the world. "You know," he said, "I've found something in religion that I never felt before. Last night I knelt by my bed as usual to pray. I've done this every night since I was a boy. When I was married forty years ago," he continued, "my wife and I agreed to pray together every night. We would kneel by the side of the bed and she would pray out loud. I couldn't do that," he explained. "And anyway she was so much better at it and I always felt God would listen to her." Rather shyly he said that he would take his wife's hand as she prayed and like two simple-hearted children she would lead this strong husband of hers up to a kindly God who must have looked with delight upon them, judging from the way he blessed them. "Well," he went on, "we did that all these years and then—then he took her away and last night I knelt down alone. Out of long habit I put my hand out for hers but her hand was not there. It all came over me then how I missed her and loved her and I wanted her so badly I could hardly bear it. I felt as I did long ago when I was a boy and scared and wanted my mother. I put my head down on the bedside and I guess for the first time in my life really prayed. I said: 'O God, I've heard about people really finding you, and I believe you do help people. You know how much I need you. I put my life in your hands. Help me, dear Lord.'" He turned from his story and looked me full in the face and his eyes were filled with wonder as he said: "Do you know what happened? Suddenly I felt a touch on my hand, the hand she always held. It was a strong, kindly touch and I felt a great hand take my own. I looked up but could see no one, but all the pain seemed to go out of my mind and a great peace came into my heart. I knew that God was with me and would never leave me." And as I listened I knew it too. Again I saw the wonderful miracle of faith whereby a man, a good man but one to whom religion had always been a formality, under a great sorrow break through into the area of spiritual power and win over a crushing adversity.

Real Christianity is very wonderful and there is no power equal to it when it has full control of a personality. By it any problem can be solved. The question might be raised, "Can it deal in similar effective fashion with the affairs of the world?" The answer is, it can do so if enough of us will have genuine faith in it and utilize it in our social problems. We need no other social program nor method, for none that we might devise would have the qualifications or force possessed by Christianity. All we need is more real faith in the Christian method. We hear a great deal today about world peace and social justice and the preservation of Democracy, and these problems are critical and vital. We flounder about from one idea to another, and many voices are raised, calling attention to themselves as possessed of some wisdom especially designed to solve these problems. Thinking and discussion are of great value and should be encouraged, but I am sure that after the last word is said and the last panacea has been analyzed we will have to return to the New Testament for a way to a better world. Only one Man by his wisdom and resources has the authority to say, "I am the way." There is one verse in the New Testament which holds the secret. Think of the trouble we would save ourselves and the number of conferences and speeches and election campaigns we could be spared if we would simply take this secret and put it to work. We have laid great stress on certain ethical teachings of the Master, and rightly so. We have felt that if we could persuade people to adopt these ethical principles, peace and justice would inevitably result. Perhaps so; and the effort should be persistently maintained, but why do we neglect another aspect and quality of religion which has been demonstrated in practice as having unmeasured power beyond any strategy man's poor brain may devise?

In the New Testament we read these electric words, "If ye have faith" (not a vast amount of faith but real faith) "as a grain of mustard seed, ye shall say unto this mountain (what a disparity—a grain of mustard seed pitted against a mountain!), Remove hence to yonder place, and it shall remove." That is not all of this amazing verse—"And nothing," (yes, that is what it says) "and nothing shall be impossible unto you." That is about as inclusive and unqualified a proposition as it would be possible to imagine. One may seek to explain it or interpret it, but there it stands in nowise watered down. It is a man-sized, straightforward, take-it-or-leave-it promise. Why do we shy off from it? The reason is, it requires more faith than we possess. More's the pity, for the few times that such faith has been exercised it has astounded the world with its results. If we could get even a few people to embrace and live on this mustard-seed faith, we could utterly revolutionize the world in the name of Christ, putting all actual and would-be dictators to flight, and establish peace, prosperity, and democracy so firmly it would take years of political bungling and religious compromising to undo. Our hope today is in no political or social program. The next election, whoever wins, will not save us. Our hope, our future, our destiny lie in getting a few real people to stake their all on the workability of the faith that moves mountains. Remember what eleven Galilean peasants once did. Remember what three men, Charles and John Wesley and George Whitefield, once did. Remember what one business man once did. He lived in New York City in 1857, the year of a great panic. He listened to speeches and read articles and voted for men who were supposed to know how to save the nation. Finally, he decided that God ought to have a chance. He announced that on a certain day in a certain place in Fulton Street he would pray about the country. He "met" first alone. Then a few joined him. Soon the room was crowded. Other meetings, crowded by business men, sprang up in other parts of the city. The movement spread like wildfire to other cities. The noon hour in business districts from coast to coast saw the streets deserted as business men prayed together in faith that God's power was available to the nation. The result—the great spiritual awakening of 1857, which brought in its wake one of the most thorough religious and business revivals in American history.

We have been unable through our own efforts, despite all our cleverness, to get the nation out of the doldrums. Meanwhile religion of the mountain-moving variety has decayed very largely into formalism or ethical programism. The people who ought to lead give little attention or serious thought to spiritual values. They do not even go to church, but argue aimlessly on country-club porches. Meanwhile God patiently waits in the shadows for a few real people to believe in him and consecrate themselves to him so they can become channels through which he may pour his vast power to transform a nation from defeat and near chaos to victory and new life.

We have power in our hands to save our generation and we do not use it. This is the supreme tragedy of our time. When I say that the apparently insoluble problems of today can be solved by religious faith, my conviction is based on no idle fancy or wishful hope, but upon the scientific fact that what has happened once can happen again. It has been done and therefore can be done. Consider an historical parallel.

In 1805 a man named William Lloyd Garrison was born. He grew to young manhood, and taking a straight look at human slavery said he did not like it. He said it was wrong and announced that he meant to destroy it. People laughed at such bumptiousness, and when they tired of laughing, they sneered and said Garrison was a fool. They pointed out that slavery was a great mountain in human history, an ancient, firmly planted institution. It had existed from the dawn of civilization. The great empires of Egypt, Greece, and Rome had been built on slave labor. Single individuals owned as many as ten thousand slaves. The English-speaking world had long recognized slavery as a basic institution, blessed by religion. When the Peace of Utrecht was signed in 1713, which gave England a monopoly on the West African slave trade, the treaty was celebrated in Saint Paul's by the singing of a *Te Deum* written by the Christian composer Handel especially for the occasion. In America slavery was likewise firmly established. In 1835 the governor of South Carolina declared: "Slavery is the cornerstone of our Republican edifice. Destroy slavery and you put a stop to all progress." The same principles were held in the North. A professor in Yale University said, "If Jesus Christ were now on earth, he would, under certain circumstances, be a slave holder." In 1855 the Moderator of the Presbyterian Church declared, "God has permitted slavery for wise reasons." At the time of the Dred Scott decision most of the members of the Supreme Court were slaveholders. The law honored it, the Church blessed it, business profited by it, and the nation recognized and practiced it. It was a mountain, as granite is a mountain, and who could destroy it?

Garrison said he could. Garrison believed in God with the faith of a child. "I trust in God," he said, "that I may be his humble instrument of breaking at least one chain." He became the most hated man of his time. He was ostracized and burned in effigy, but he went up against the mountain. He was a man aflame. His biographer declares: "The continuousness of Garrison is appalling and fatigues even the retrospective imagination of posterity. He is like something let loose. I dread the din of him. I cover my head and fix my mind on other things; but there is Garrison, hammering away till he catches my eye and forces me to attend to him. If Garrison can do this to me, who am protected from dread of him by many years of intervening time, think how his lash must have fallen upon the thin skins of our ancestors. The source of Garrison's power," declares his biographer, "was the Bible. He read it constantly. It was with this fire that he started his conflagration."

So, armed with faith that nothing could daunt, Garrison rolled up his sleeves, took his little hammer of mustard-seed faith, and approached the great mountain of human slavery. He brought down his little hammer and a faint tingle was heard. The people laughed and booed and sneered. But Garrison brought it down again and again. Blow after blow fell until his little hammer became a great sledge, the reverberations of which could be heard throughout the land. As he beat with his faith upon the mountain, a crack began to show. It widened until the people shouted with a mighty voice, "Look, the mountain is breaking!"

The glorious, thrilling fact is that just fifty-eight years after Garrison was born, human slavery was outlawed forever in the United States of America. It is an illustration of the shining truth that any mountain can be broken down by faith when men are completely surrendered to God. We can end war, depression, moral decadence, social injustice, and restore declining democracy if enough of us, like Garrison, will take seriously these words, "If ye have faith as a grain of mustard seed, . . . nothing shall be impossible unto you."

There is still another area where Christianity must give power to win in life if it is to measure up to the place we have assigned to it. It must help you and me as individuals to overcome ourselves. We have been discussing the method for solving the intensely perplexing problems of society. It would perhaps be easier to accomplish that feat than to solve the intricate and complex personality of one man's own self. If you are like most of us, you are yourself the most difficult person with whom you will ever be forced to deal. Every man somehow must come to terms with himself. That is not easy of accomplishment. There is a perverse element in each of us, and in some it constitutes a real problem. Every right-thinking and normal person wishes his better nature to prevail. No man consciously wants to live life on a low or inferior spiritual level, but there is something in us that prevents us from being what we want to be. It is the fact that our whole nature has not been brought under God's control. There are still pagan areas within us. These unspiritualized elements of our lives get us into trouble.

Miss Muriel Lester, the distinguished social worker of England, tells of an old woman who was frequently in her cups. Miss Lester labored with her in an effort to help her gain control over herself. It was discouraging business, the futility of which seemed to impress the old lady herself. One night after a spree, hearing

Miss Lester's kindly admonitions, she cried out in be-
wilderment, "Miss Lester, God never made a better
woman than I am, but I can't live up to it." So may
it be said of many of us. Saint Paul stated the same
dilemma in more classical phrase, "O wretched man
that I am, who shall deliver me from the body of this
death? The good that I would I do not; but the evil
that I would not that I do."

Here is a man who found the answer. He was a
successful executive and enjoyed a plentiful supply of
money. He was what might be called an "up and out"
in contrast to the common phrase, "down and out."
Without money, he would have been the latter, for he
was the victim of his own sins. He was, it seemed, in
an almost continual state of partial or complete in-
toxication and there was no restraint to his habits.
He came into contact with some people who had themselves experienced the restorative powers inherent in
Christianity and the ancient and astonishing miracle
of new birth took place in this man to the end that
there was a complete change in him. Now, Sunday
after Sunday I see his radiant face in the congregation
and behold a man who knows the meaning of triumphant living. I heard him say one day, "I would not
give one day out of this new life for all of my past
experience." And I knew that a man who could look
as transparently happy as he did at that moment
meant what he said.

CHAPTER II

THE ART OF SELF-MASTERY

WHEN I was a small boy living in the city of Cincinnati, one of the high spots of each summer season was our annual trip up the river to *our* Coney Island. What a time of excitement as we boarded the old *Island Queen!* With her decks full of happy youngsters she would steam proudly upstream, her side wheels stirring the muddy Ohio. On the top deck the calliope was playing a lively air and occasionally the deep-throated whistle would reverberate among the Kentucky and Ohio hills to the delight of small boys, some of whom have never forgotten it.

At Coney Island, among the many diversions, was one called "The Maze," so named because it was a veritable jumble of passageways. The idea of the thing was to find your way out once you had gotten in. This was exceedingly difficult, for, in addition to the intricacy of its construction, the walls and floors and ceilings of the maze were made entirely of mirrors. As you turned expectantly down passageway after passageway, seeking elusive exit, everywhere you went you ran into yourself. The place at every turn seemed blocked by a figure and that figure was always yourself. At every point all you did was to collide with yourself. It was a most bewildering experience, but later reflection and the realism of living show it to be only a diminutive model of the world at large. This world has indeed the qualities of the old Coney Island "maze," for wherever one turns in this life he will run into himself. One may think his problem is other

35

people or conditions or circumstances, but he is likely
to discover that his essential problem is himself.

Take the question of happiness. If one is dissatisfied and discontented and unhappy, he may be con-
vinced it is because of outward conditions or other
people. But when he actually and realistically sets
himself to find his way out of his unhappiness, he runs
into himself. It is surprising how little a man's outer
life need govern his inner spirit when he is the integrated master of himself. By the same token it is
amazing how little outward material circumstances
contribute to happiness when one is at loose ends in
his inward life. I sat one day on the veranda of a
palatial home with a man worth millions. The
grounds, stretching away in cultivated perfection, were
exquisite and lovely. Every material value was available for elegant and gracious living. One would expect to find here no worry or anxiety or any of those
annoyances so common to the average run of humanity.
Surely, in a setting like this any man would be happy
and contented. Yet, strangely enough, this man is
one of the unhappiest persons I have encountered in
all my experience. Sitting there in the cool of that
veranda, he poured out a stream of dissatisfactions
sufficient to move a heart of stone. It was a beautiful
sunlit afternoon and the sunshine sprinkled down between the leaves onto the close-clipped velvet green
lawn beneath. The breeze gently stirring the leaves
caused their delicate shadows to move about on the
grass. Staring at them he said: "See the way the shadows chase themselves around under those trees? That
is one of the few things which give me comfort. They
did it just like that under those same trees when I was
a boy and," he sighed, "when I had a good time living."
It required no expert in the vagaries of the human

mind to know that the trouble with this man was that
shadows were chasing themselves around in his mind.
He had lost control of his inner life. The peace and
serenity of his mind had been dissipated by the thinness
of his intellectual and spiritual life and no amount of
outward luxury and relief from monetary trouble could
compensate for that. His trouble was with himself.
In the maze of life he had run into a dead-end inter-
section and collided with himself.

Take also the matter of our everyday human relationships. If you make up your mind to like a person,
it is remarkable how likable that person can become.
If you fill your mind with friendliness, it is astonishing
the number of delightful people one will find in the
world. But if your heart is crabbed and irascible and
filled with suspicion and dislikes, it is surprising the
number of unpleasant people on every side. To a
large degree you make the kind of people you meet by
what you are within yourself. In other words, in your
personal relationships you very definitely run into
yourself.

I know a woman who deals everlastingly in vague
and shadowy implications about people. She never
directly says a condemnatory word but her inferences
for that very reason are all the more devastating. A
lift of the eyebrow, a knowing look when a name is
mentioned, and a seed of suspicion is sown. There
must be something wrong with that person, you decide,
and because your information is veiled in mystery,
the slander is the greater. It is an effort to avoid
having one's judgment of people colored by such a
mendacious and subtle style of gossip. I began to feel
there was something wrong with everybody in the community. I knew there must also be something wrong
with me too, for you can always be sure that a person

who will gossip to you will inevitably gossip about you. The more I began to know people in that community, the more I discovered that they were as fine folk as one could find anywhere. The trouble was not with the people; it was with this woman. What she imagined wrong with others was, in most part, a projection of what was actually wrong with her. When one's personal adjustments to other people are unsatisfactory, the first solution should be to make an honest analysis of himself. In every phase of life the principle is valid. Most of our difficulties are within ourselves. At every turn a man runs into himself.

The greatest skill in which one can become proficient is to learn the art of self-mastery, for at every turn (and there are not a few every day) you will find a figure with which you must deal, and that figure is yourself. Some people who acquire skills and techniques and who manage to attain what appears to the world as success are still unhappy and dissatisfied, and the reason is they have not learned to control and organize themselves. Sometimes those who have achieved the most in culture, wealth, and honor have been the least successful in the art of living.

In my office some time ago I saw this illustrated. One of my visitors was an eminent professor of philosophy. He knew the great thoughts of the great men of the world. He had worked out an adequate system for the explanation of life. But he had gotten his own life into a terrible muddle and as a result was unhappy, disillusioned, and dissatisfied. My other visitor was a simple, elderly woman who had never had any more schooling than the three R's—reading, 'riting, and 'rithmetic. She knew nothing about philosophers. Her knowledge of the arts and sciences and history was very limited, but one thing she had discovered in her seventy years of hard life was how to have peace and happiness in her heart. Her face showed she was at peace with the world and found life good. It would seem she was a greater philosopher in a practical sense than the philosopher himself.

All of this is by way of saying that it took me, personally, a long time to learn one great lesson about life—and the lesson I learned is this, which I sadly confess to you, that most of my troubles and failures were caused by one man, and that man is myself. I have found myself to be the most annoying, distressing, and disturbing person with whom I have ever had to deal. Of course, like every other human being, I have tried to lay the blame elsewhere. I have blamed other people. I have blamed conditions. I have blamed my friends. I have blamed my long-suffering wife. But when I have been honest with myself, I have had to confess that I myself am the cause of ninety-nine and forty-four hundredths per cent of my troubles.

Now that we are finished with me, let us get down to you. What is true of me is doubtless true of you. You are probably the one who is constantly getting in the way of yourself. Many years ago Emerson, a very wise man, put into his daily journal the following note: "Henry Thoreau made last night the fine remark that as long as a man stands in his own way, everything seems to be in his way—government, society, and even the sun, moon, and stars." Yes, that's the trouble with most of us. We get in our own way.

A constant stream of people passes through a minister's study in the course of a year. Some people think a minister does nothing but preach a sermon on Sunday. That is only a part of his work. He spends the rest of his week consulting with people about the most difficult personal problems of life. We deal every week

of the year with people who have sinned, who have
failed, who have lost control of themselves—people
discouraged, haunted by fears and worries, people who
are trying to get a new grip on life. It is well that
people do come to the minister about all of these
problems, for though we ministers may not be the
wisest men in the world, we have a medicine that works
when taken. But what I started out to say was that I
have discovered that the problem of nine out of every
ten persons is to be solved in their own personalities.
Any man who is honest must admit that if he could
solve his inner conflicts and problems, he would very
largely solve his outer conflicts and problems. No
truer statement was ever made than the immortal lines,

> "The fault, dear Brutus, is not in our stars,
> But in ourselves, that we are underlings."

Omar Khayyám's well-known discovery is a universal
one among honest men:

> "I sent my Soul through the Invisible
> Some letter of that After-life to spell:
> And by and by my Soul returned to me,
> And answered 'I myself am Heaven and Hell.' "

Goethe says, "Beloved brother, let us not forget that
a man can never get away from himself." Therefore
it is a great thing when an individual finds the secret
of getting release from himself.

If a man can never get away from himself—a fact
indubitably real to most of us—the only remaining
alternative is to master himself. The art of self-mastery is not easily attained, but its accomplishment
makes a man of you, and its results far outweigh all
the effort involved. So great is its value that the wisest
of all books tells us that he that ruleth his spirit is

better than he that taketh a city. If Chiang Kai-shek, the commander of the Chinese forces, should retake Shanghai from the Japanese, the world would applaud the exploit. If you can learn to conquer your own spirit and master yourself, you have accomplished a bigger thing than that, declares the Bible. Yes, self-mastery makes men. No man can become great or even efficient in the highest sense without conquering himself. Obviously, all his personal force must be under control and contributing to his effectiveness. The reason many people end up in a place in life below that for which their natural endowments seem to qualify them is because their inability to master themselves has resulted in the dissipation of energies, faulty concentration, and a generally soft impact against problems, instead of the incisive, unified attack a controlled self makes possible.

As strong men are made by learning self-mastery, so are the qualities of gentle beauty. Real women, for example, who possess the rarest charm and beauty are not those who weakly acquiesce in the shoddy standards of a crude, pagan society. On the contrary, the loveliest women are those who have ideals and will stand for them, come what may. Not the least of the attractiveness of such a woman is her delightful uniqueness. Most people have not the stamina or strength of personality to be different, but those who do and in a gracious manner (and this is an art in itself), acquire a charm denied the common run who, being of the herd, ape the herd. The most utterly hopeless statement any woman, or man either, can make and which brands them with a futile finality is the ultra excuse, "But they all do it." The fact that the unthinking, dumb following, mob does a thing in nowise endows it with value. On the contrary, it is likely to brand it as quite common. That person is distinctly worth while who can "be himself" against the pressure of custom to which weaker persons yield. The worth-while person has the poise to think his practices through on their merits and also the fine, clean-cut nerve to look the herd (I use this term to cover the social set also, often the most subservient herd of all) full in the face and announce that one intends to live his life according to fine, clean standards, and is totally unconcerned by the opinions of anybody, if such mass attitudes as we have today can be characterized by the honorable and courageous word "opinion."

The art of mastering oneself involves the conquest of fear and discouragement and other phases of the emotional life, and we deal with them elsewhere in this volume. Here we shall consider two specific problems of fundamental importance—how to win in the area of our habits and the technique of overcoming wrong impulses. Both of these matters have been amazingly and profoundly involved in determining success or failure in the lives I have observed.

When I was a student some years ago in the city of Boston, I passed daily by a statue of Abraham Lincoln in Park Square. It represented two slaves kneeling be-fore Lincoln, who was in the act of striking the manacles from their wrists. It is a notable work of art, a moving and tender human story in enduring bronze. The suppliant attitude of the freed slaves, the look of gratitude on their faces, the strong strokes breaking the chains, the kind look on the face of the emanci-pator, always made me feel what a great thing it is to break the chains which bind human beings.

But there is a far greater chain-breaker than Lincoln. Once long ago a Man had acquired sudden and con-siderable fame in the country where he lived. He came back to his home town and stood up to make a speech, and in that speech made this immortal statement—"He hath sent me . . . to preach deliverance to the captives." From that day to this history has resounded with the clangor of chains falling from the captives to whom Jesus Christ has given freedom. But the kind of chains I am thinking of now and which are referred to in this statement are not chains shackled on by tyrants. I refer, rather, to the thought Charles Dickens had in mind when he said, "I wear the chains I forged in life." In life we do forge for ourselves many chains by which we bind ourselves and become in strict truth captives with freedom lost. Of all these chains with which people sacrifice their freedom and sovereign power, habit is one of the most common and most pathetic. As a clergyman, I have the inestimable privilege of entering rather intimately into people's lives. Again and again we run into the problem of habit. Many times have I heard the question raised— "Yes, but how can I break bad habits and form good ones?" I have heard that question so many times and have seen its importance so often that we should frankly face the problem of overcoming bad habits and forming good ones.

What, then, is the solution of this common human problem? What is habit? Habits, good or bad, have their origin in the tendency of the nerve centers to duplicate or repeat their impulses. It is important to note that it is an acquired tendency toward the repetition of an act or thought. We are not born with habits. A child, newly arrived, has no habits whatever. He only begins to have habits when he learns to do certain things and perform certain acts. When he has done them enough times so that they become automatic and are done, therefore, as we say, "by second nature," they have become habitual. A baby learning to walk, at first has to watch every step and is necessarily awkward. As the days pass and he continues to practice the art of walking, the time comes when he can leap and run and give no thought to the movement of his limbs.

This automatic quality of habit is illustrated by what sometimes happens when you think about an action which you have performed for a long time. A man dressing himself for the day will be thinking of many things as he ties his necktie. It is an habitual act. Let him begin, however, to analyze how he should tie his tie and often it is necessary for him to stop and get his mind on something else until the habit grooves begin to function normally again. There is the classic story of the old gentleman who had a long beard. One day a friend asked him whether he slept with the beard on the inside or on the outside of the covers. He tried to think and was finally forced to say he did not know. That night when he retired, he at first put the whiskers under the covers, but that did not feel comfortable. Whereupon he placed them on the outside of the covers—and that looked silly. He finally became a nervous wreck trying to decide where he did put them.

The first thing, therefore, in our thinking about habit is to understand that it is an acquired tendency which becomes a fact due to repetition. This means that one can be master of his habits, discarding and selecting them as he desires; if he is willing to practice the kind of life that breaks chains and sets captives free. If you are struggling with a habit, it is important that you understand that the habit is not inherited nor laid upon you by some dead hand, but that you have acquired it yourself by repetition over an extended period. I have consulted eminent physicians who substantiate the statement that there is no reason, because a father had certain bad habits, why his son should assume that those habits have descended to him by heredity. They have been made easier for him to adopt, perhaps, by environment and example but there is little evidence to indicate that habits are passed down from generation to generation through hereditary strains. As already remarked, when you were born, you had no habits. As you observed people about you there may have been a tendency for their habits to become yours, but they became yours only because you practiced them yourself. The great truth is, therefore, that you can be freed from any habit that is wrong or harmful and from which you want release.

Before we deal with the actual technique of breaking bad habits and forming good ones, it may be helpful to know something of what this involves. Old habits, naturally, are the hardest to break. They have made deep marks on our nervous system. The old habit has cut its path and therefore its movement is swift and easy. The new habit is forced to blaze its trail through our personalities, and it is slowgoing. A simile might be that of the pioneers in the early days cutting a trail through the woods. At first it was exceedingly difficult business, blazing trees, cutting them down and making roads, and at that stage it would be easy to form bypaths or new roads altogether, but once the trail had been cleared and a road built, movement over it became free and easy, and it became habitual for people to travel that way. An old habit has a smooth, well-worn highway through the nervous system and a new habit has to blaze a trail slowly through the wilderness of a man's personality. This is especially true of habits learned in childhood. Relax under certain circumstances and there is a tendency to fall into old ways, for the old road is still there, overgrown a bit perhaps, but still waiting for you. I discovered this by a simple incident some time ago.

I was brought up in a Middle-Western city where the distance between two streets is referred to as a square. If one should ask you how far it is to a certain place, you would say, perhaps, "Three squares." I have lived for many years in the East where the distance between two streets is referred to as a block and here in New York City, if I were asked how far it is to a certain place, my quick rejoinder might perhaps be, "Three blocks." Some time ago I found myself in the city of my infancy, standing on the corner waiting for a member of my family. A pedestrian asked me how far it was to a certain place and my instant reply was, "Three squares"! It is an illustration of the fact that under certain conditions of environment the old habit tracks assume control of our thinking.

This fact of one's human nature should serve as a particular warning to young persons to be cautious about the kind of habits they develop. When an action becomes automatic, it is exceedingly difficult to break it if it is a bad habit. This is especially and tragically true of habits that produce a morbid craving in the nervous system, such as the use of alcohol and similar narcotics. The most important scientific as well as spiritual truth that can be impressed upon young people is—If you want your life to be happy in the years that are to come, do not allow yourself to form any bad habit. By the word "bad" I mean any habit that is destructive of personality or of physical values. Let a man once get into the grip of a habit and often it is only by a terrific battle that he throws it off, and unless he wins the fight it may sweep him to destruction.

I was at Niagara Falls recently on a beautiful sunlit afternoon. Far above the falls the river flows along peacefully and placidly. One would think no danger lurked there. It is simply a lovely river flowing between the green banks of a peaceful countryside. But as one proceeds along the stream the current becomes swifter and more tenacious, and there is finally a point beyond which, if an individual proceeds, no power on earth can save him. He is inevitably swept to his doom. He is caught in the grip of a mighty current. You and I have seen people caught in a current like that—a habit that gripped them and held them fast. They cried out piteously for release, but they were swept on over the brink into defeat and ruin. They were deluded by the subtle fact that at first the sin looked comfortable, and they said with a laugh: "There is no harm in this. Besides I can stop any time I want to stop." The answer is that up to a certain point you can perhaps stop, but you will reach a point at which, if you continue, the friendly sin becomes your bitter enemy. Robert W. Service, who knew as much about sin as any preacher, describes it in an unforgettable couplet:

> "It grips you like some kinds of sinning
> That turns from a friend to a foe."

This may sound like old-fashioned advice, but it is earnestly substantiated by modern psychologists and psychiatrists. Anyone who deals with human personality as it is knows that the wise young person will be very discriminating in the kind of habits he allows to be formed in his life.

But how shall one break a bad habit and form a good one? One way is to give a bad habit no sustenance—that is, cut off its food supply. To use another figure, give it no exercise. If you know what it is that excites the stimulus of a bad habit, cut off the stimulus by suppressing the cause for it. Here, for example, is a person who has the bad habit of making mean or sarcastic remarks. He has a lot of pet hates. He naturally is led to associate with people of a similar mean and sarcastic type. Walter Winchell says with rather shrewd understanding of human nature that a good many people could say their friends are those who hate the same people they do. The process of starving this bad habit is to cultivate people who have a kindlier attitude. Stay away from people who by their own irascibility stimulate the bad habit of gossip. An added help is to cultivate a stronger desire for the opposite trait—in this case, kindness—so that the old habit will gradually drop completely out of consciousness as it is replaced by the new and greater desire. A person who wishes to overcome the habit of drinking, for example, would do well to stay away from company where this habit is practiced.

It is also well not to attempt to overcome bad habits by direct or frontal attack. Thorndike, the eminent psychologist, says: "It is the error of all of us to fight useless battles, useless because, being weak, you are very likely to be beaten; being strong, the victory is gained at too great a cost. We must remember the nervous system and the reactions it has built up." The secret of overcoming bad habits is not to steel one's will and say, "I will overcome this if it kills me." One must come at this, rather, by an act of displacement, by filling the mind full of something else. The whole personality must be geared to new impulses, new ideals, new hopes and dreams. One must cut off everything that has fed the bad habit in the past. One must disassociate himself from every idea or association that has stimulated it, and take into his mind thoughts and ideals and impulses which move in another direction. The French writer, Abbé Dimnet, suggests in this connection that we set apart a certain time each day— say, between certain hours, few at first and increasing them as we grow stronger—to refrain completely from indulging the habit we are trying to break. Gradually we shall grow stronger, and the number of hours may be increased, until at the end of a few months we shall have become completely free from the domination of the bad habit we are seeking to conquer. Another real help at this time may be found in the cultivation of a new hobby or skill, one that is all-absorbing.

But the great and only sure solution in this matter of breaking old habits and forming good ones is found in religion, by association with Jesus Christ, by living with him, by putting one's life in his hands until one is changed inside. Christ has a wonderful power to eradicate old habit grooves. Christ is an expert pathfinder in the wilderness of a man's personality, helping him to blaze new habit paths. When a person follows Jesus Christ, the scientific explanation of the change in him is that he is no longer feeding or exercising a bad habit but is causing it to atrophy and therefore grow feeble and finally die because of lack of nourishment and use. But over and above all this—the fundamental explanation of overcoming bad habits is that God does it for one by an act of grace. One of the greatest phrases in all the world is "the grace of God." Simply stated it means: A man has no power in himself; he is weak; his will is weak; he wants to gain a victory but does not have the strength. Then he turns to God, confesses his weakness and humbly asks God to give him strength. He is humble and contrite and out of God's great mercy this man, who has no strength, is given power far beyond that which he needs, so that he has it now to spare. Faith in Christ has demonstrated itself no end of times as being stronger than the effect of man's nervous system. No matter what your habit may be, how deep the grooves may go in your personality, if you put your life by an act of surrender into the hands of God, you will receive power equal to your need and will be able to overcome the bad effects of your acting and thinking through the years, that which we call habit.

Henry Drummond, distinguished preacher of a bygone generation, Dr. George Truett tells us, was riding many years ago over a mountain road with a driver who had been reduced from an eminent niche in life because of his inability to overcome a bad habit. Drummond, with his kindly desire to be of help to all human beings, soon had the man telling him the whole story, and heard him sadly declare he could not overcome this bad habit in his life and acknowledge that it was taking him nearer and nearer to complete ruin. "What can I do, sir?" he said to Drummond. "Suppose," answered Drummond, "that this team of horses should suddenly become frightened and run away and this carriage should go careening around these mountain turns and we were in great danger. Suppose you knew that I was the most expert horseman in the realm, well able to handle any horses, however wild or out of control, what would you do?" The coachman said, "Why, sir, I would instantly put the reins in your hands." Drummond said: "Certainly, and why don't you put the reins of your life into the hands of the great Expert in human nature. You cannot overcome the habit by yourself. Why don't you let Christ take the reins of your life?" The man saw the point and came to that most important of all spiritual decisions, as a result of which he gained control of his life and overcame his habits. This can happen to any man who is willing to ask for and yield to the grace of God.

Whatever our needs may be, if we will bring them to Christ, they can and will be solved. Christ can do anything for us if we will only let him. For one thing, he can give us the power to win over our temptations. What a fair world this would be if we could defeat the temptations which assail us! To know that moral struggle had at last resulted in final victory would be as deep a satisfaction as life can produce.

What a strange assortment of emotions and impulses and hereditary strains and environmental influences a man is! He is of the earth earthy, possessing feet of clay, but again and again we are reminded that he also has divine qualities. He is both good and bad, strong and weak. Ideals appeal to him, stir him deeply, and forever lure him like the gleam of lights on far towers, but at the very same time sin attracts him, temptation urges him, until he finds himself in the grip of a terrible conflict which grows out of his very nature.

One of the best descriptions of this dilemma in the personal life is a verse which represents the homely philosophy of a British soldier:

> "Our padre, he says I'm a sinner,
>   And John Bull, he says I'm a saint.
> But they're both of 'em bound to be liars,
>   For I'm neither of 'em, I ain't.
> I'm a man, and a man's a mixture
>   Right down from his very birth;
> And part of him comes from heaven,
>   And part of him comes from earth."

This conflict, which each of us must recognize as exist-ing within himself, may be solved and peace attained;

and the secret is to learn to effectively handle our temptations, for temptation is the decisive point in the battle. The result of our struggle with temptation may determine in a large degree our happiness and well-being in life. Without question, the one chief cause of human misery and unhappiness is the fact that people yield to temptation and commit sin. Men usually make their own unhappiness, and it is because they do evil instead of good. It would be too much to say, perhaps, that all unhappiness is caused by sin, but the fact is that most of the deep, dark misery in men's lives is caused by sin.

In my experience I have often had reason to reflect upon a curious fact—that the deepest and most profound philosophy of life is not found in the great thoughts which famous thinkers have set down on paper, but often in humble and simple people is that wisdom which truly enlightens and inspires. Perhaps because being philosophical by nature, and living close to the main stream of life, they have had deeply practical truth revealed to them. Thus Calvin Coolidge sat at the feet of an old cobbler in Northampton, whose shrewd and kindly observations gave to the famous Vermonter some of that quality which endeared him to a nation. Thus Lincoln, leaning over the counter of a country grocery store in conversations with the farmers and woodsmen, filled his mind full of that homely wisdom and practical understanding of human nature which enabled him to deal with all sorts of men in the critical days of the Civil War.

I recently had occasion to witness the truth of this principle, sitting in a shoeshining parlor. While the proprietor of that institution worked on my shoes and I read the paper we discussed various items in the news—among other matters a crime which was then prominent in the public print. We were led into the query as to why such things happen. Giving a flick to his cloth, the shoeshiner opined, "I have noticed that in all these affairs somebody or some people were doing what they should not be doing and," he continued, "most people get into trouble simply because they do not behave themselves." Then he concluded with what I regard as a wise piece of philosophy: "If you do right," he vigorously declared, "usually things will be right." I was struck by that and it occurred to me it had a strangely familiar ring. It did not sound quite original and I felt I must have read it somewhere, so I went home and got out an old Book in which I have found more wise truth about the business of living than in any other source. Sure enough, there it was—and this is what I found: "And thou shalt do that which is right and good in the sight of the Lord: that it may be well with thee, and that thou mayest go in and possess the land which the Lord sware unto thy fathers." In effect, what the Bible is saying is that if you do that which is right and good in the sight of God, it will be well with you and you will come into possession of the good land—which is to say, the good life. Do right and life will yield to you its richest fruits. This old writer of the book of Deuteronomy stated a truth which wise men in the common run of life in every generation discover by hard experience—that if you do right, things will be right.

The shoeshiner was right, and we have seen the truth of his philosophy illustrated scores of times. In my interview room, just the other day, sat a man broken nervously and physically as well as financially. Once he was a strong, vigorous, successful business man, president of a nationally known organization; now he

is on the scrap-heap, and why? He could not overcome temptation. He fell, and his life fell in on him.
Sometimes a preacher is asked why he always harps
on sin. The answer is because every day of the week
in the sacred and confidential relationships he has
with all sorts and conditions of men he hears the
tragic story of lives that might have been happy and
successful had they not yielded to the temptation to
do wrong. This is no pious parsonlike theory with
which we are dealing, but the saddest everyday fact
in human life. Many people who will read this book
know from sad personal experience that what I am
saying is all too true.

This was borne out for me by another incident
some months ago. It happened that I was sitting in
the lobby of a quiet hotel in a certain city. I became
conscious finally of a conversation on the other side
of a pillar. The lobby was so quiet it was impossible
to avoid hearing what was said. I gathered that a sales
manager had met one of his salesmen by appointment
at this place and was rather severely taking the latter
to task for his failures. The salesman was making
all manner of excuses and among them was weakly
pleading for a new chance because of his wife and two
children. It was apparent that the trouble with this
salesman was not lack of ability but lack of moral stability. Curiously enough, these two men represented a
liquor concern, and it appeared that one of the faults
of the salesman was that of drinking as well as some al-
leged dishonesty. The sales manager was not what one
would call pious in his remarks but, in effect, what
he was giving the other man was a good sermon.
Among other things he said to the deficient salesman:
"The reason men fail is not a lack of ability. It is
just that they won't do the right thing." And he de-

clared, "I wish I could make you see that your success will lie in being upright and honest and truthful and in clean living." It is a long way from the old writer in the Bible to this sales manager—one is ancient, one is modern—but he was using the same old principle laid down in the words, "And thou shalt do that which is right and good in the sight of the Lord: that it may be well with thee, and that thou mayest go in and possess the land." So, you see, it seems to be an old, old story in human life, in the modern world no less than in former times, that they who do right and good find it well with them.

How are men's careers affected by their failure to do right? Do things go wrong if they do wrong? Is it well with men who do right? Do they possess the land? It is important to consider this, for there has been a general softening of standards of late years. It has affected the youth of the nation. Our American youth is basically strong and good, but I wonder if they are being taught high moral standards as in the past. Many of us were taught the old maxim—that honesty is the best policy. That may have had a utilitarian ring to it, but it was true just the same. The honest man came out best in the end. That does not mean that he had more money than the dishonest man but he had, at least, the respect of the community and the approval of his own conscience, and that is worth a great deal more than stocks and bonds and motor cars that you have no right to. Of late years the phrase, "Get away with it," seems to express a pretty common attitude or general philosophy. It may even be considered a bit old-fashioned to emphasize that to do right is the best way to happiness and well-being, but how can we help but emphasize it if we are going to talk about the truth, for it is absolutely sure that people who do right are the happiest people? In our jails and courts, and in every other place where human trouble is aired, most of the people we find there are paying the penalty for doing wrong. Run down the list of the happiest people you know, people who are genuine, glad to be alive and who get the most from living, and you will find that they try to live according to the best standards they know. It is a deep-dyed fact of the universe that if a man does wrong consistently, everything for him has a tendency to go wrong.

I remember sitting late at night not long ago in a roadside hamburger stand, eating a sandwich with a young fellow who had asked to go with me some short distance to another city where I made an address. We had stopped on the way back for a bite to eat. During the long evening in which we had driven together over the hills in the moonlight he began to unburden and tell me about his life. It seemed to be a series of one false move after another. It was full of sin too. It was a dark, sad picture that he gave me. We got up to continue our journey, and I shall never forget the look of desperation on his face as, standing by the car outside the road-stand, he said—and I quote his actual words—"Everything I do goes wrong and I know the reason. The reason is that I am wrong myself." You can't run away from that. This may be coming to you from a preacher, but preachers are men who see life in the raw. They know what people do and they know how they suffer for it, and they know that a man who commits a wrong is likely to have it hound him, putting its bony and tragic finger into everything he does, to his undoing.

But there is another and glorious side to this story. There is One who can help us win over our temptations, and that one is Jesus Christ. In first Corinthians we read: "There hath no temptation taken you but such as is common to man: but God is faithful, who will not suffer you to be tempted above that ye are able; but will with the temptation also make a way to escape, that ye may be able to bear it."

The method for overcoming temptation is, therefore, to fill your mind and heart full of Christ's spirit. Build up within your mind and soul good and noble thoughts. The Freudians tell us that evil thoughts come up out of the unconscious mind to torment us. But if you put good and clean and noble thoughts into your conscious mind, by and by your unconscious mind will be saturated with those thoughts so that it will send up, not evil impulses, but good. In a deep sense you are what you think. Before you do an act with your hand, you do it with your mind. Think bad and you will do bad. Think good and you will do good. The sinister fact is that if you do a thing often enough with your mind, you will do it with your hand. The mental thief is very likely to become the actual thief. The mentally impure is likely to become the actually impure. Emerson said, "The thought is ancestor to the deed." "Think of evil and," says William James, "down among the nerve cells and fibers the molecules are registering it, storing it up against us when the next temptation comes."

In a certain state a family had operated the bank in a small town through three generations, and the family had an honored name. Then came the great depression and the young banker, being financially overextended, was hard pressed for money. One night all alone in the bank the thought came to him that falsifying the books offered a way out. He resolutely put the thought from his mind, but it returned again and again, the resistance becoming less vigorous until one night his hand finally performed the deed with which his mind had dallied. Against this could be told story after story of men similarly tempted, but who had spiritual reserves which came to their aid, and their temptation was repulsed. That was because they had taken Christ into their lives, filling their thoughts full of his grace until they had developed within themselves spiritual power and moral strength sufficient to meet any crisis. In them a temptation was destroyed as a moth is frizzled up by a flame.

If a person will adopt the policy of thinking about Christ, repeating some of his words and offering a prayer in his name now and then during the day, he will find that this simple practice will fortify him in a most effective way against the attacks of temptation which come when least expected. If you will surrender your life each day into the keeping and protection of Christ, you will build up within your personality an immunity to temptation so that you can meet it and control it, for it will have no power over you. Spiritual vitality in you will be too strong for temptation to break down. You can win by the art of self-mastery.

CHAPTER III

HOW TO GET ALONG WITH PEOPLE

THE manager of the leading hotel in a large city extended a rather unusual invitation. He asked me to come to his hotel and speak to his employees. He promised to relieve every possible one of his workers from their responsibilities and assemble them in the Grand Ball Room for half an hour. "What is the purpose of the meeting and on what topic do you desire me to speak?" I asked. "Oh," he said, "say something to get them ambitious, something to make them want to amount to something. Even give them some religion," he concluded desperately. He explained that he was troubled by the lack of desire for advancement in the young people of ability who were working for this great hotel corporation. "They have their eyes on the clock," he declared, "and are apparently more anxious to get away from the job than to do the job well. As long as they get enough to support themselves and go to the movies and a dance now and then they seem perfectly contented. It's a shame to see young people satisfied with something less than they have it in them to be," he argued. But the point that struck me about this curious meeting to which I was invited was the statement of his real purpose. "Tell them how to get along with one another," he requested earnestly, and explained: "I have to fire more people because they can't get along with their associates or their superiors than for any other cause. Seventy-five per cent of our dismissals are for this reason," was his amazing statement. This hotel man, who was not a church man, felt, and soundly, too, that religion could help in a problem which I later learned is one of the most practical considerations in the success or failure of most of us.

The point of view of the hotel man was confirmed some time later when at a banquet I was seated beside a gentleman who employs hundreds of men in his industry. Our table conversation turned to what many regard as one of the unfortunate by-products of the contemporary relief program. We shared our common conviction that every American should be spared, by social responsibility, the privations of depression times. I found in this leader of industry genuine concern for the hardships of our fellow Americans everywhere as a result of the troubles that lie thick upon us. He also expressed his anxiety about the future ruggedness of the American character, particularly in the oncoming generation, because of the not always wise paternalism which becomes an abuse of relief expenditures. As he spoke, a recent incident of my own experience crossed my mind. A young fellow, long out of work and on relief, asked me to assist him in securing a job. By a stroke of rare good fortune I found an opening and was told by the employer to have the boy report for work on Monday at nine o'clock. It was not much of a job, paying only a modest wage, but it was a chance to do honest work and turn an honest dollar, and good men and true have been doing just that through all our country's history. Late Monday morning the employer telephoned the information that the young fellow had "not showed up." I sent word to the boy and had back the eloquent reply that he had thought it over and concluded he could "get about as much on relief without working for it." I told him later with a restraint upon which I really prided myself that people who expect the world to give them a living may eat and find shelter, and all will agree they should have it, but as for Success, they will never win her favor or know the meaning and deep satisfaction of achievement won by man-sized effort and skill.

This high-minded business executive, who has himself risen by courage and toil from poverty to a position of eminence, turned a bewildered face to me. "I can understand poverty," he said. "I was born in it and have always hated it. I will help any man to lift himself out of it, but I cannot understand any young man so lacking in red-blooded manliness. I would follow a plow again if necessity required it," he declared, "and be glad of the chance." Looking at his square jaw, I knew I was looking at one of those real men who made America and that he meant what he said. Most Americans like this are only one generation removed from the factory and the farm, only one generation from overalls to tuxedos, and they have not lost the knack of labor and struggle nor a deep, fundamental sympathy with it. I referred him to an article by the late Newton D. Baker, one time Secretary of War, on "The Decay of Self-Reliance." In his article Mr. Baker tells of a young man who came to him seeking his influence to gain admission to the Dominion of Canada that he might spend the winter trapping fur-bearing animals just south of the arctic circle. Mr. Baker reminded him of the rigorous conditions of that territory, where temperatures for long periods range from sixty to eighty degrees below zero. This fact seemed in nowise to deter the young man, who pointed out that he had previously trapped animals in northern Maine. Then with a very quiet smile on his face he said, half apologetically, "I suppose you think I am a little crazy, do you not?" And Mr. Baker replied: "I wish I could tell you what I really think about you. I am wondering whether I do not see in you the last survivor of the pioneer. I wonder whether you are not, in fact, the last young man I shall ever see who is not afraid of the dark and of hardship, and wants to stand on his own feet and force his own way by the vigor of his own spirit and the strength of his own hands." Mr. Baker continues: "I gave him the letter he wanted. Perhaps as I write these sentences he is setting his traps amid accumulating winter. In any case, I am thinking of him and remembering that of all the young men who have come to see me in the last two or three years he is unique. All the others, in one form or another, have come to ask me how to get the government or some philanthropy or somebody else either to direct them or to provide for them in return for sheltered service against the hazards of individual enterprise."

"I know," my dinner companion declared with satisfaction, "there are many left like that courageous young fellow, and with men of that quality we shall work our way to better days wherein we shall have not only material prosperity but more real justice for all men."

But this is only one angle of the conversation I set out to report. I asked this employer, "What, in your opinion, is the secret of success?" He cited several factors that he thought were involved in success. Then he added, "I can tell you the reason not for success but for failure of a great many people." He continued, "I think that more people fail because of defects in human relationships than for any other reason." In other words, in this man's opinion, most people fail not because of a lack of ability or of training or education or opportunity, but because they do not know how

to get along with people. When we think of people
we have known and honestly consider our own lives,
I wonder if it isn't true that the inability to get along
with people has been responsible for failure many
times.

Here is a man in business who never seems to make
progress. Either he is going constantly from one job
to another or he never forges ahead in his own company. Other men come up from the ranks beneath
him and are elevated above him. He remains always
a cog in a machine. What is his principal trouble?
It may be, of course, that he is not properly trained,
or his home environment is not helpful, or he is not
physically well—all of these things enter in, but is it
not true in many cases that he never advanced because
he is a friction point in the office? He does not seem
to mesh himself into the smoothly running machine.
He is a jarring note.

I think of my own profession, the ministry. Some
ministers have a strange record of brief and stormy
pastorates, a year or two in a church and then they
have to move on. What is the trouble? Lack of consecration or ability? Usually not. A minister complained to me once about his church. He said the
people were very difficult to get along with, and then
went on to say, "I think the church at large is made
up of very difficult people." He cited a long string
of churches he had served, telling about all the unpleasant people he had dealt with. Some time after
that I met one of his official men and in discussing this
minister the man said: "He thinks we did not like him
because his ideas are 'progressive,' but he is wrong.
We are not opposed to honest thinking even if we do
not always agree with it. The trouble with him is he
always rubs people the wrong way. His trouble is

not his ideas; it's the way he says things and does things."

What is the secret of getting along with people? I shall endeavor to answer that question in a practical, workable way. First, a good plan is to take an active interest in the other fellow. Most people are naturally interested in themselves and do not want to hear you or me talk exclusively about ourselves or our interests. There is no greater bore than the man who talks constantly about himself. If you want the other fellow to be interested in you, talk to him about himself and forget yourself. Interest yourself sincerely in his problems, his achievements, his hobbies, and he will like you.

I was a reporter once on a newspaper in the Middle West and among my calls I had to see a police sergeant for news relating to that department. He was a formidable old fellow, grim of visage, and had a bark designed to scare all young reporters out of their wits. It was like bearding a lion in his den to talk with him. I found he had a little granddaughter, however, and soon realized she was his weakness. One night I surprised him by saying, "How is that nice little granddaughter of yours?" He melted like snow in the springtime and became a fast friend. Interest yourself in the other man. It is the simplest form of psychology.

I am not a regular reader of Dorothy Dix's column but I sometimes glance at it with real interest. I observed some time ago a note from a young woman asking Dorothy Dix the plain and open question as to how she could induce a certain young man to propose to her. I thought the answer she gave was sensible. In effect she replied that the best way to get a husband is to talk to a man about himself. That is a good thing to remember if she begins to talk to you about yourself; it is barely possible she may have designs! The same strategy has been known to work on the fair sex also. Manifestly, I am not suggesting that one should take an active interest in other people for selfish reasons. It is a fine habit of mind to cultivate and is an open door into lasting happiness, but it is also true that if in a desire to get along with people, you practice the principle of taking an interest in them, after a while you will come to have a genuine love for people and, as Abou ben Adhem learned long ago, love of our fellow men is about the highest rung of life's ladder.

A prominent business man, head of a famous American corporation, explained his method of success. He started in life with nothing. He was so poor it was impossible to go to school. Now he is president of the Board of Trustees of a large university and the recipient of honorary degrees. He said, "I have learned life's lessons not from schools but from people. Every man," he used to tell me, "has something I can learn from him." I have noticed he is a great listener. The other man is always encouraged to do most of the talking. This man listens. He takes the values other men have to give and uses them to enrich his own life. In this process, however, he has not only gotten much for himself but has acquired a genuine sympathy and understanding for other men, so that he has become a great benefactor of humanity and is justifiably beloved and respected. To get along with people and be successful in life, forget yourself and learn to love and be interested in other people. Sincerely strive to help them all you can, and having cast your bread on the waters it will certainly come back to you.

Another important factor in human relationships is the power of self-control. The man who gets along with people is the man who can receive slight and injury and not get mad about it. A business man said, "You can always measure the size of a man by the size of the things that make him mad." It is a mistake, a great mistake, for any individual to wear his feelings on his sleeve. The man who knows how to handle people is the man who does not lose his temper. The controlled man is the powerful man. Everyone has a temper. It would be unfortunate if one did not have a temper. Temper is to an individual what it is to a steel blade. It adds quality to steel and to men. But a temper must be under control. The problem is whether you will control your temper or your temper control you. The little man, the man who fails, who never succeeds, loses his temper. He says sharp things. He talks first and thinks afterward. He loses his friends. He makes enemies. He dissipates his influence. He fails. The big man, the man who succeeds, thinks twice before he speaks, does not speak, or else speaks softly—and wins.

The classic example of a man who got along with people because he knew how to control himself was Lincoln. Think of the men this woodsman came among! He came up from the backwoods to the Capitol, to the seat of power, where he was surrounded by the most cultured, highly educated, ablest men of his time. They had a low estimate of him at the start. They thought he was a crude frontiersman. William H. Seward, Secretary of State, early in Mr. Lincoln's administration came to him one day with a letter saying: "Mr. President, we have been in office four weeks. Some one must establish a policy." This meant that I, Secretary Seward, will fix a policy and you, Mr. Figurehead, will carry it out. A little man would have been insulted. He would have said that somebody was infringing on his prerogatives. Mr. Lincoln, however, in a quiet way showed Mr. Seward that he knew what he was doing, that he appreciated advice, but without saying so indicated that he was the master. Seward, who knew a man when he saw one, a few weeks later said, "The President is the best man among us."

Secretary Stanton once spoke of the painful imbecility of Mr. Lincoln. Instead of retaliating, the President showed the Secretary of War every consideration and when he died, Stanton said that Lincoln was the greatest ruler of men in all time. He got along with people because he knew how to control himself. He knew how to forgive; he knew how to be long-suffering. He received the taunts, the slights, the insults, the hatred, and yet he treated all men with kindness, with firmness, with love. Where did he learn this art? I never look upon the tall, lank form of Lincoln that I do not see behind him the form of another Man, a Man nailed upon a Cross, a Man who said of his enemies who had nailed him there: "Father, forgive them, for they know not what they do." Ah, there was a Man who knew how to deal with people, a Man who two thousand years after he lived is the most beloved Man in the world. You can win in life, but it is certain that to do so you must know the homely everyday secret of getting along with people.

One point at which many fail in personal relationships is in their reaction to criticism. It may appear to be a curious irrelevance, but have you ever considered the difference between a man and an oyster? Obviously, there are many points of contrast, seemingly an entire disparity. Presumably a cynic might be able to note some startling resemblances between the two. The point of difference I have in mind is that the oyster was created with his skeleton on the outside and his nerves on the inside. This marks him as a low-grade animal because he has small capacity for suffering. Man, on the contrary, has his structure in reverse of that—his skeleton is on the inside and his nerves on the outside. There is a significance in this difference. It has both an advantage and a disadvantage for man. It makes possible his boundless progress. The higher the capacity for suffering, the greater the development of the creature. Man is the most highly organized of all creation. Civilization in large part stems from the effort of man to reduce his suffering. He suffers from the cold, and over long centuries his active mind invented means for overcoming this difficulty. He suffered from disease, and the development of medical science resulted.

But this capacity for suffering likewise creates the problem of sensitiveness. Man's nature, being sensitive, may be inspired by beauty but it may also be hurt by unkindness. His mind, being sensitive, may be responsive to great ideas, but it may also be wounded by opposition and antagonism. His personality, being sensitive, may open to love as a flower to the sun, but for the same reason it may close to hate as the flower fades before the chill winds of autumn. Because man is what he is he must deal with the situations arising from his highly organized and sensitive nature. One of the most common of these problems is what to do about criticism. His attitude toward criticism, both that which he receives and gives, will have its effect on how well he gets along with people and ultimately his ability to win in life.

Criticism is quite common. We have to take account of it every day. Tomorrow someone will criticize your work or your dress or your manner or something you have done or said. You know the words, "I like him and would not say a thing against him for the world, but did you hear this or that?" For this actual dilemma of everyday life, Jesus Christ has the answer. His principle of turning the other cheek or adding the cloak or going the second mile works out with superlative skill in human relationships. The person who actually seeks to base his attitudes on the principles and spirit of Christ gains even more than workable technique. He receives into his soul a power that lifts him to a height where criticism can be handled with fine control. It endows him with that calmness and philosophical detachment of spirit by which, for example, he can skillfully discriminate between worthless and valid criticism. That ability requires a quality of Christian patience that will not allow one to be emotionally disturbed by criticism to the extent that he can no longer think or act with cool rationality. The failure to do so has disastrous effects on our relationships with other people. This faculty is truly a gift of the Spirit, an act of God's grace. It is interesting how every problem of life can be solved when one puts his life in God's hands, seeking to live his way and trusting God for help. Those who make real contact with Christ thenceforth possess an inner greatness which lifts them above the petty conflicts which once caused them to fail.

Fortified with this inner grace, one can view his critic with imperturbability, asking simply whether he is competent to criticize, accepting and profiting by the criticism if he is, dismissing it if he is not. Fritz Kreisler, master of the violin, for example, would be very foolish to become upset if I were to criticize his playing and he were told about it, for he should realize that my musical knowledge is so inferior that he should pay no attention to it. Business men with this grace

will not allow themselves to be agitated by the criticism of people who know nothing about merchandis-
ing and meeting a payroll or any of the problems of
business. Analyzing criticism in the far height of
Christian urbanity, one realizes that much of it ema-
nates from unworthy motives such as jealousy, vindic-
tiveness, or the desire to curry favor with those who
are presumed to feel as the critic feels. You know this
type. "What do you think about someone?" he is
asked. "Well," he counters, "what do you think?"
Then when he is sure of his ground, he proceeds with
his sharp knife veiled in simulated friendship to cut
with criticism.

This quality of inward grace will help one to receive
valid and well-meant criticism graciously. For sincere
and honest criticism any man should be appreciative
and he should be able to take it in good spirit and
profit by it. The worth-while man, the kind of man
who makes the greatest success, never loses his humility.
He knows there is much he can learn and is ready and
willing to learn from anyone. Some people find it
hard to take criticism even from their friends who sincerely love them. Their resentment sometimes flares
out in petulant anger. More often it is ostensibly received as given but results in a cooling of friendship.
For this reason some people never receive criticism of
the friendly kind. They are recognized as "touchy"
and accordingly are allowed to remain in their own
conceits. People do not like this type of person very
well because it is uncomfortable to have him around.
One never knows when the wrong thing may be said
in his presence, causing his sensitive suspicion to flare
into unpleasantness. To be able to receive justified
and unjustified criticism from friend and foe alike is

a mark of moral greatness. Think of the real Christians you know and you will observe that this quality is a result of their close relationship with Christ. He bestowed upon them this greatness of spirit. Real Christians, being wholesome, square-shooting, friendly, kindhearted, strong-charactered human beings, have the rare gift of getting along as far as is humanly possible (to leave the loophole dignified by Saint Paul) with all men.

One cannot, however he may steel himself, handle the problem of criticism effectively by self-control. Soon or late his will power will give way under pressure or when off guard, and a sharp word or ill-concealed resentment will result in what may easily be an unfortunate incident. But even if one should by strength of will always preserve self-control, it is at great cost to the nervous system, which is compelled to inhibit anger and ill will that would ordinarily find relief by outward explosion. Retained within, it creates tension. Neither of these methods is satisfactory. The happy and truly successful procedure is to get aboard that power that will lift you above yourself and fill your soul with kindliness and strength.

A life story which admirably illustrates this victory of the human spirit is that of John Wesley. His is one of the most thrilling biographies in print. If ever a man was hated and maligned, misunderstood and criticized, it was this great preacher of the eighteenth century. He was refused permission to speak in the churches. He was insulted by epithet when he stood in the open air to preach. He was spat upon like his Master. Like the saints of old, he was stoned and mobs sought his blood, but through it all, year in and year out, he carried on, re-enforced by an inner power until by the sheer beauty of his spirit and the power of his gospel he became the greatest and most beloved man of his age.

Some time ago in England I came upon an entrancing story. The saintly Wesley one day was preaching in a downtrodden section of London, a place where raucous and ribald pleasures held sway, a sort of deteriorated Coney Island. Wesley was addressing a vast multitude of people when, over at the edge of the crowd, two ruffians appeared. They said to one another: "Who is this preacher? We'll show him. What right has he to come here, spoiling our fun?" They reached down and took a stone in each hand and belligerently elbowed their way through the crowd until they came within hailing distance of the preacher. Then they drew back their arms with the stones, ready to hurl them on his face, when as Wesley was talking about the power of Christ to change the lives of sinful men, a beauty spread over his face, that great old light never seen on land or sea, and transformed him with its effulgence. They stood transfixed, their arms poised in air. One turned to the other with a note of awe in his voice and said, "He ain't a man, Bill; he ain't a man." The stones fell from their hands onto the ground, and as Wesley spoke, their hearts were softened. Finally, when the sermon had been completed, the great preacher made his way through the crowd, which parted respectfully to permit him to pass. One of the ruffians very timidly reached out his hand to touch the hem of the preacher's garment and as he did so, the attention of Wesley was drawn to him and his companion. He put out his two hands and placed them on the heads of these two ruffians and said, "God bless you, my boys," and passed on, and as he did so, one ruffian turned to the other and said, with even more awe in his voice: "He *is* a man, Bill;

he *is* a man. He's a man like God." Wesley won by
love, which at long last breaks down every form of ill
will.

The capacity for genuine friendship is another important element in getting along with people. It will
help you to win if you have a love for humanity that
is bigger than all the small and false barriers that
usually separate people, barriers like color, creed, and
social position. The friendly man always wins friends.
The genuine, wholehearted nature possesses an infectious likability that cannot be resisted. There is
something fundamentally repellent about the selfish
person, whose thin affections are insecurely rooted
largely in what he can get out of his friendships. People
instinctively sense this insincerity and have little regard for such an individual. If the author may be for-
given for an exhibition of fatherly pride, I have a little
son two years old who is already beloved by many for
what a friend called "a million-dollar smile" and a
rippling chuckle that makes everybody laugh with
him. A wise man who is himself of large influence
said to him recently, "John, keep that smile and
chuckle, for it will see you through life." A happy,
loving spirit of good, old-fashioned, wholesome friendliness is an important element in the recipe for getting
along with people.

"I can count my friends on the fingers of one hand."
Many times we hear that statement made. It assumes
we can have only a few real friends. That is placing
an undue, and I believe an unnatural, limitation upon
the happiness and development of our lives. Lotze,
the philosopher, defines life as "To be in relations."
That is to say, one lives in proportion to the number
of points with which he makes contact with life and the
world. A man whose interest is in his business but

who also has an interest in literature, art, and religion is four times as alive as the man who is interested only in business.

A man who can name all his friends on the fingers of one hand is by the same standard of measurement only half as alive as the man who needs the fingers of both hands to count his friends. The man whose sympathies and interests are broad enough to include many folk in the circle of his friendships finds a satisfaction in life which the man of more circumscribed relationships cannot possibly appreciate.

From the point of view of one's self-interest it is the part of wisdom to have as many people as possible touch your life beneficially. Every individual can make some contribution to your development in the form of information, inspiration, points of view, or just the fine leaven of fellowship. Tennyson's Ulysses says, "I am a part of all I have met." In a more elevated sense a broad friendship makes our lives worth while by enabling us to touch and help more people.

What our country needs possibly as much as anything today is a re-emphasis on old-fashioned neighborliness. There is too much irascibility and ill will in the land, too much suspicion and antagonism between groups. This has never been a class-conscious country. Rich men and poor men, capitalists, workers and men of every walk in life have always preserved a kind of comradery which gives a distinctive flavor to American life.

I heard recently of an incident out of real life which admirably illustrates that broad tolerance and friendliness which is typically American. The spread of the spirit of this little story throughout the land would go far toward making life happier for all of us.

"Parson Tom," as he was known in the Western

town where he labored so faithfully, was killed on Christmas Eve crossing the road from the church to the manse. He was struck by an automobile steered by a drunken driver, and died almost immediately. The letter which follows was written by Joe, "The Cop," a devout Roman Catholic, who had made the acquaintance of "Parson Tom" some years ago when the latter was the pastor of the Presbyterian church in his town. The fellowship was maintained through the years, and Joe was writing his semiannual letter to "Parson Tom" when the radio announced the news of his tragic death.

My dear Parson Tom:

Once again the blessed Christmas season is with us and I am minded to write the semiannual letter to my old friend and, may I say, co-worker—"Parson Tom." Considerable water has gone under the bridge since my last letter, but I am hoping that. . . .

Over the radio comes the announcement that you have gone on a long journey. A journey to the bourne from which no traveler ever returns. But I've somehow a feeling that you'll get my letter. So—I'm going to finish it.

Water under the bridge—and bearing with it—memories. Memories of the many nightly conferences in the little study at the parsonage. Just we two—The Parson and The Cop— doping out how we might bring back into the fold some stray youngster—maybe one of your kind—maybe one of my kind.

Memories of rain-swept streets; warmth and lovingkindness inside—the hard head of the Scotch Protestant almost touching the noggin of the Irish Catholic across the library table as we groped for a way to make some erring husband remember his wife and family. Or who could we hit for a basket of groceries for some poor family.

Memories of the talks we had in the still hours of the night. Talks that would cause some of your strict churchmen to arch their eyebrows. And make some of my beloved brethren gasp.

They say you were on your way somewhere with an armful of presents when the call came. You would be, carrying the word to the last, you were. And the word is this, to my way of thinking—"Greater love no man hath than this; that he lay down his life for his friend."

You're up before the Throne. It's hard to picture bluff, smiling, tolerant Tom in the Presence. But there you are—or else all this talk of the after-life is the bunk. There you are—making a talk for some poor man—or woman—or kid needing a break.

And I'm thinking that maybe you will be dropping just a word or so for the good of the soul of

Your old friend,

THE COP.

Perhaps the principal reason we do not get along with other people is because we do not get along with ourselves. We are much disturbed by antagonisms held by other people toward us but too little concerned by the unfriendly feelings we have for them. Mr. Justice Sutherland, who recently retired, mellow in wisdom, from the Supreme Court, observed shrewdly, "Human nature is so constituted that we fully tolerate in ourselves what we condemn in others." We think the other man ought to be changed but give too little consideration to the possibility that we ourselves ought to be changed. In a deep sense that is the trouble with this whole contentious and strife-torn world. We want to see the other fellow or the other nation changed, but give little thought to the necessity for our own change. The most sinister, damaging, and deadening attitude of the human mind is its unwillingness to see its own weakness and honestly face its own faults. Get changed spiritually yourself—that is the real solution of antagonism. Perhaps the antagonisms which sprout all manner of unpleasantness about you grow out of some unchristian area in your own life. Here again the certain method by which you can win will do its work. Frankly and unreservedly surrender to Christ your whole life, including not only the cruder sins of the flesh but also the more subtle but no less reprehensible sins of the disposition. Sometimes people who have been converted from the so-called darker sins stop short of conversion from the sins of gossip, malice, jealousy, and plain ordinary irritability. Not infrequently in the case of irritability and irascibility it might be well to consult a good physician or psychiatrist, for it is conceivable that some physical difficulty or emotional maladjustment is exerting pressure which produces tension which, in turn, expresses itself in outer irritation. It is possible that the reason one cannot get along with people is that he is ill either in body or personality or both. The most frequent and common diagnosis, however, is that his illness is spiritual, and only one Doctor can handle that case. Only one Physician can compound the medicine required. Turn to that Physician, take that medicine, and I assure you that without the shadow of a doubt a change will take place in you that will change the attitude of all worthy men toward you. A young man, who was constantly in "hot water," to use his own words, came to talk about his troubles. He was a capable young chap with lots of ability, splendid education, and a really delightful personality, when he was pleasant, which was the rub in his case. He managed to get jobs but not to hold them for long. He complained about every job, saying his associates were "impossible," to use his word for it. Somebody was always trying to turn people against him, it seemed, and the boss favored others over him. I investigated and found that a peaceful and harmonious office organization seemed always to develop friction points shortly after his arrival. It was difficult to analyze specific instances, for often they were not altogether tangible. He seemed to cause agitation all about him. One employer said simply that he was a "trouble-maker" and declared: "The only thing to do with a trouble-maker is fire him. It's no use and a waste of time trying to straighten him out." Another man said our young friend "had good stuff in him" and could rise in his business but was hopeless unless he could learn not to "rub people the wrong way."

Having both sides of this young man's picture, it was evident some serious straightforward business had to be done. The only alternative was failure, unhappiness, and a wasted career. With all possible kindness I led him to see that he was self-centered, egotistical, touchy, and stubborn—in a word, that his own spirit was wrong. He was a clean-cut fellow morally, a fine ethical Christian. The trouble was his ethics were Christianized but not his spirit. He recognized the accuracy of the diagnosis. He was not one of those weaklings afraid to be honest with himself, nor did he seek to evade the issue by specious rationalization. He faced the issue like a man. "What must I do about it?" he asked. "Give your whole personality, including your spirit, to Christ," I answered. This he did with a whole heart. Christ, who never fails a man who is in earnest, took from him his selfishness and egotism, softening his spirit, endowing him with forbearance, understanding, and kindliness. The finished product is a co-operative, likable, gracious—and, be it said—successful Christian man. He knows of a truth that you can win when you learn the real secret of getting along with people.

CHAPTER IV

GOD AND YOU ARE UNCONQUERABLE

GOD will do anything for you that down in your heart you really want him to do. God will do for you anything you will permit him to do. He will actually give you strength, peace, happiness and boundless well-being if, deep down in your nature, you sincerely want these advantages and desire them enough to take them. We fail to possess these boons, not because they are beyond us or because life is cruel; but because something within us throws up a strange barrier beyond which they cannot pass into our lives. Many people are in the pathetic condition of needing something, wanting something, and being offered that something, but are seemingly unable to take it. The reason they cannot take it and are thus denied the inestimable joy of life, is due to no outward failure or to any lack in God's love, but, rather, to a tragic fault within themselves. To put it in a word, they want spiritual power but down deeper they do not want it. They are caught and held fast in a sad dilemma. Therefore they do not get it, for their real desire is negative. The pity of it is so many do not understand why.

It all sounds most confusing and intricate, does it not? It is just that, and the reason is that you and I are intricate and confusing in ourselves. The most difficult person in all the world to understand is one's own self. A vast number of tributary streams feed the main current of our lives. Meandering streams they are, often with their sources hidden in mystery, which flow in from the back country of heredity, racial and biological areas and childhood experiences, as well as from the immediate environment. Socrates admonished us to know ourselves and Tennyson assured us that self-knowledge, along with self-reverence and self-control, leads to sovereign power. But to know oneself is a difficult undertaking. Schopenhauer, lost in meditation, bumped a man in the street. The man in irritation said: "Look where you are going. Who are you anyway?" To which Schopenhauer, ever the philosopher and stopping short to conjure with this question, said, speculatively: "Who am I? Ah, I would that I knew!" It is strange but true that we have never even seen our own faces. For some of us that should probably be cause for comfort, but the fact remains that no man has ever looked directly upon his own countenance. He has, to be sure, seen a more or less accurate reflection of it in the mirror or a representation of it in a picture, but has never seen the real face. It is too close to him for that and the character of the physiognomy will not permit it. It may also be said that one has never accurately heard his own voice as others hear it. He hears a sound with many of the voice's true qualities, but the full voice, recognizable and always familiar to those who know him, is denied its possessor. Coming from a recent radio broadcast, an employee of the station told me he had just made a recording of our program. He invited me to listen to it. He put on the record and I listened to an address I had made only ten minutes previously. It was an amazing experience. I was listening to a man making a speech—a man whom I scarcely seemed to know. It was a strangely unfamiliar voice. Needless to say, it was an humbling experience to hear oneself as others hear him. Two or three times I caught a tone that sounded much like the voice of one of my brothers, but for the most part I was hearing a voice and getting impressions of a personality quite unfamiliar to me.

A recognition of the fact that we need to know more about why we do what we do will help us become what we want to do and be. I want to call your attention to a quotation from the world's greatest book on psychology, or the science of understanding the human mind. This quotation may help us considerably in our effort to master the technique of winning in life. The reference is found in the New Testament in the Gospel of John, chapter five. I shall quote it exactly as it is written there:

"Now there is at Jerusalem by the sheep market a pool, which is called in the Hebrew tongue Bethesda, having five porches. In these lay a great multitude of impotent folk, of blind, halt, withered, waiting for the moving of the water. For an angel went down at a certain season into the pool and troubled the water: whosoever then first after the troubling of the water stepped in was made whole of whatsoever disease he had. And a certain man was there, which had an infirmity thirty and eight years. When Jesus saw him lie, and knew that he had been a long time in that case, he saith unto him, Wilt thou be made whole? The impotent man answered him, Sir, I have no man, when the water is troubled, to put me into the pool: but while I am coming, another steppeth down before me. Jesus saith unto him, Rise, take up thy bed, and walk. And immediately the man was made whole and took up his bed and walked."

This is the story of a man for whom something tremendous was done. Let us see what there is of value for us in this incident. First of all, it had to be decided by this man whether he really wanted to be healed. In the light of our modern knowledge of disease the possibility exists that this man was what we call a neurotic person. The distinguished religious psychologist, Leslie D. Weatherhead, of London, holds to this interpretation.[1] By a neurotic is meant one who is making a faulty adjustment to life. In order to escape unpleasant factors in the business of living, or some difficult responsibility, the mind slips into a faulty adjustment. While doing this the mind often shuts off from the consciousness the fact that an imperfect adjustment is being made. Thus the neurotic thinks of his reactions as entirely normal and does not know he is making such a faulty adjustment to life. Going still further, the mind can set up definite physical symptoms of illness to relieve the neurotic from the necessity of unpleasantness or responsibilities which he dislikes or of which he is afraid. The mind sets up these symptoms of illness to preserve the self-respect of the person by enabling him to tell himself that he is too ill to face these disturbing factors. It is a trick of the mind to save one's face. Let me illustrate.

I heard of a woman who had one son whom she loved very much, perhaps too much, for her mind rebelled against the idea of ever sharing his love with another. It was "smother love" rather than mother love. It so happened, therefore, that when he developed an interest in any young lady, on the evenings when he had engagements with the girl, the mother would often develop very bad headaches or actually be forced to bed. The son would then have to telephone and cancel the engagement. He had to stay at home and hold his mother's hand instead of the hand he had hoped to hold. When he finally became

---

[1] *It Happened in Palestine,* p. 157. The Abingdon Press.

engaged to be married, the wedding had to be postponed three times on account of the recurring illnesses of the mother, which always seemed to clear up when the marriage was delayed. Finally the son decided to brave all consequences and proceed with the marriage. The mother became, to all appearances, very ill, but when the wedding was over, she quickly recovered. This mother was not consciously pretending illness and, as a matter of fact, her symptoms were probably real enough, but her mind was forcing her into this faulty adjustment due to her abnormal mothering of her son.

So possibly in the case of the man at Bethesda, his mind had finally brought him to a condition where he was utterly defeated. He lay helplessly about among the lame, the halt, and the blind. Moreover, he had done it for thirty-eight years. Surely in all that time somebody would have helped him into the healing waters. If he had been in earnest, he could have crawled to the brink of the pool, balancing himself there until the moment arrived, and have fallen in. Christ came to the pool and, looking upon this man, saw through him in a moment. He observed that here was a case of the will to fail. Accordingly, he looked this man full in the eyes and in a kindly but stern tone said, "Look here, my friend, do you really want to be healed?" Never has there lived anyone with the sure and skillful insight into human nature to equal Jesus. The look in the kindly eyes, the stern demand upon his consciousness, the electric vitality in the very presence of Jesus broke through the prison which the man's mind had built up all those long, helpless years. At last he was revealed to himself. For the first time in his life he really wanted with all his heart to be healed, and when, in tones of ringing authority, Jesus said, "All right, if you really want to be healed, you don't need anybody to put you in the water; stand to your feet like a man and walk," the man stood up radiant in his new-found strength.

So we who need strength from God and want it after a fashion must decide whether we really want it badly enough to take it. How glorious to realize that if we really want the great things God can give us and tell him so, meaning it with all our hearts, we shall hear him say, "Arise and walk away from every crippling, unhappy thing which has deprived you of spiritual power"! Today, wherever you are reading this book, Christ draws near and puts to you the question, "Do you really want to be healed of your difficulty? Do you really want to be better?"

Suppose your problem is a quick temper or a mean disposition. You wish you did not have the tendency to say mean, sharp things, but you are constantly catching yourself doing just that. You would like to be delivered from this fault, you say, and at times you mean that, but if you are completely honest, are there not times when you at heart do not want to be changed in this regard, for it gives you a sense of power? "We tell them a thing or two," we say. "Nobody can put anything over on us," we boast. "I told him where to get off," we report with simulated satisfaction. This ministers momentarily to our ego. It compensates for our feelings of inferiority and inadequacy, but it leaves us spiritually at low ebb. We know there is much more happiness in the virtues of kindliness, humility, and love. A man's spirit can become a thing of beauty and his relationships may be free from turmoil and friction if he wishes it deeply enough to take this gift of God's grace. As we point out elsewhere in this book, no person with a mean spirit or sharp, unkind tongue can win in this life.

It is probably more difficult to make a mean person into a kindly one than to transform a gross sinner into a saint. The man whose sins are those of the disposition comes much more slowly to the crisis of his moral sickness, the point where he realizes his sinfulness. He thinks because he is not guilty of the sins of the flesh or dishonesty or lying and other offenses of similar nature that he is "pretty good." Thus we have some irritable and unpleasant Christians who stand in need of a conversion of the disposition. It has always interested me to note that in the parable of the prodigal son both of the sons were sinners—the one, low down in the flesh, as E. Stanley Jones puts it, and the other, high up in the disposition. One was an out-and-out sinner. While not in the slightest sense condoning his sinfulness, at least we may say of him he was what he was. The other boy was perhaps a crabbed, formal churchman, who sat with hard face and hard heart in the family pew on Sunday. (They are few and far between, far less in number than the skeptical, ungodly suppose.) He probably passed the collection plate and gave the worshipers a chilly feeling as they beheld his wintry face written over with pious complacency. Undoubtedly, he was on the session or consistory or official board, although he did not deserve to be; that is the place for spiritually-minded men; and his chief interest presumably would be how the money is coming in. For my part, if I had to choose between the older and younger brother for a golf partner some summer day, my choice would be the younger brother; for, bad as he was, he was at least a human being with blood, not ice, in his veins. He might swear a bit, but he would count all his strokes, and maybe we could get him to quit his swearing. It is significant that it was this younger brother who at length mended his ways, for he knew he was doing wrong, and when a man knows that fact you can reasonably entertain hopes for him. The older brother thought he was "all right," and with subtle and skillful touch, the mark of masterful writing, the last we see of him in this drama in the Bible is as the same unregenerate fellow who entered the story. He was still in his "far country" of the disposition.

The tremendous thing about Christianity is that it can change even people like this when they sincerely desire such a change. Any person can be healed of the mean disposition that holds him back from happiness and success if he sincerely wants this blessing enough to take it.

In a certain community lives a man of benign appearance and gracious demeanor who is beloved by an entire city. He is a man large of stature with corresponding largeness of mind and spirit. In business he occupies a position of outstanding responsibility. In attempting to describe him one always finds the word "powerful" wanting to be used. His sympathies, interests, attitudes, and convictions are all of them on a big scale, and one has a feeling too that his emotions, like anger and pugnacity, might also be violent, were they not under control. That, of course, is the point; they are under control. A master hand holds them in check. But it was not always so. Once this was about the meanest, hardest, and most violent personality in town. He was always precise in his ethical standards. He was ever within the moral law. Sin of the gross or fleshly type was no problem for him. He was a member of the church and an impeccable observer of its outward rules, but in him was no Christian kindliness. His heart was frozen. He was as hard as nails. He extracted the last ounce of flesh in any deal. There was in him none of that charity which overlooks a fault because it believes something better is in a man. At times the deep fires within his volcanic nature would burst forth in frightful anger in which, during the explosion, unbelievable malice and hatred were revealed. The dark evil of cruelty that was almost sadistic was unleashed with a force that made him the most feared and disliked man in town. Then a miracle occurred. A minister came to this man's church who talked a new brand of religion, or, at least, it seemed new to those who listened, but in reality it was the old kind in the thought and speech forms of contemporary life. This minister, they soon discovered, had something deep and powerful in his own heart, which bubbled out of him like an overflowing spring. It had an infectious quality, this message of his. There was nothing labored about it, no obvious effort to preach showy or intellectual sermons. Indeed, people lost sight of the preacher, who was himself lost in the act of taking something hot and burning out of his soul and putting it into the hearts of his people. Folk who used to loll apathetically in the sparsely filled pews, expecting to hear only the same old words, now sat bolt upright, caught by an inspiration they had not felt in years. Something throbbed in these sermons like a lost chord they never expected to hear again. The pews began to fill up, nor was it because anything sensational was being preached. These sermons were simple and human, interwoven with homely humor and sprinkled with tears. They had the common touch. Unconsciously he was following Browning's wise injunction, "Would you have your songs endure; build on the human heart." They

were straightforward too. There was plenty of sand-
paper in them, nor were they ever lacking in courage.
The social note was there without compromise, but
these messages dealt with men's common life. Men
listening to them found comfort in their troubles,
hope in their discouragement, and the reality of God
as the companion of the daily life began to grow upon
them. At times the minister reminded them of one
of the old prophets, thundering against their sins.
He revealed them to themselves and the revelation
startled them. At other times the tones were tender,
calling them with a strange lure to a higher and finer
life. Under this preaching Christ became a live, vibrant figure, so near they could almost hear the sound
of his voice and see the beauty on his face. One by
one the people opened their hearts and gave their
lives to this Christ. People were being made over in
this place. People who had thought they were living
real life according to their cocktail pagan mode now
saw the paucity of that. They discovered in this kind
of religion that one can outlaugh, out-enjoy, and be
thrilled by living, to a degree that makes cocktail
lounge existence stale and insipid. The contagion of
religious experience was making a new community.
In the midst of this warmth sat our icy-hearted, mean-
spirited friend. But the fires were too warm even for
him and his heart began to melt. The minister
formed a friendship with him, for this minister was
a masculine sort of fellow, who sincerely liked this
rugged giant. Gradually the big fellow's heart opened.
Royal soul that he was, when he did a thing, it was
not by half measures, and one day he said: "Parson,
I'm a pretty poor Christian. You have something and
I want it." Conscious of the wrong in his life (conviction of sin, they used to call it) he was now like a

little child in the spirit, ready to be taught. Before this, in his conceit, he imagined himself good enough and so further advance in spiritual truth was impossible. The minister took him over the path he himself had followed to his own deep experience. Down that path this rough giant met a great Figure, who touched his personality with the alchemy of his skillful fingers, drawing out the spleen, the malice, the hatred, and pouring into his soul his own tenderness and love. The result was a miracle of God's grace—a new creature. Now a great kindly man walks noble and inspiring among men. That is wonderful, isn't it? That is why this author believes so enthusiastically in Jesus Christ. He has seen the Master do the most amazing things with the most unlikely people. When the man in this story, who had doubtless often wished he might attain finer control over his disposition, finally wanted that to happen with all his heart, his desire was fulfilled. God will do for you what down deep in your heart you really want him to do. You can win, but only with positive, never with negative desires.

Suppose your problem is one of fear. You are ceaselessly haunted by worry and anxiety. You are worried about money, about business, about your children, about your health or that of your loved ones. Do you realize it is possible for people to live with fear so long they are afraid to give fear up? They hate it and want to be released but are afraid to accept freedom because, strange mental quirk that it is, they are more at home in the narrow prison house of fear than in the spacious palace of freedom.

But you can be free from fear. You can escape from it completely so that it no longer haunts you or in any sense dominates you. This very moment, while you are reading this book, if you want this freedom

sincerely, tell Christ so and if you really mean it and
have faith in him, you will hear him saying, "Arise,
take up your bed and walk" away from your fears.
Do not lie helpless with your fears by your pool of
Bethesda, missing the joy and satisfaction of fearless
living. The failure of many people is that, having
made this declaration to God, they expect some overwhelming emotional experience to happen in spectacular fashion. God sometimes works so, but usually
he operates in an undramatic, though no less effective,
manner. When you were a child and awakened
frightened in the night, you called your mother. She
comforted you and quieted your fears with the words,
"Don't be afraid; mother is here, nothing can harm
you." Into your childish heart came a great peace
and you turned over and were soon in deep sleep.
Why? Simply because you believed your mother.
You had utter confidence in her. When as an adult,
you take your fears to God and want with all your
soul to be free from them, just realize that he is saying,
"Come unto me and I will give you rest." "Perfect
love," we are told, "casteth out fear." That means
perfect confidence too, just as it did when your mother
cast out your fears as a child. Simply believe that God
has taken away your fears, not that he will do so tomorrow or next year or sometime in the future, but
now. Cardinal Mercier, whose life reflected it, said the
secret of serene power is "to give yourself confidently
to the goodness of God." If you do so, like the man at
Bethesda, you will be freed by Christ this very minute
from your fears. Genuine desire and complete confidence is the secret of winning. With that secret God
and you are unconquerable.

Suppose your problem is a sin, secret or open, like
impurity or perhaps dishonesty in one of its many

varieties—dishonesty with words, with money, with love. We pray for and certainly desire purity and honesty of mind and conduct. But there are other times perhaps when one loves lust more and the mind secretly delights in that which is evil. Even the finest people have to exercise vigilance to keep the mind under control lest sinful desire creep in insidiously. When one commits a sin, the mind instantly tries to justify it or to rationalize it. Today there is less protection for the individual who wishes to live according to a high moral standard because society, on the basis of its looser morality, attempts to justify the sins men commit. The way to offset it is to fill your mind so full of spiritual vitality that this natural tendency to rationalization may be overcome. Another procedure —and it is this to which I want to direct attention—is to bring yourself to the point where you really want to be free from sin. People continue to sin for only one fundamental reason, which is that they want to do evil more than they want to do good. The late Doctor Parkhurst, of militant crusading fame in a bygone generation, quaintly philosophized on the slow progress of society: "The good people," he explained, "get tired of being good faster than the bad people get tired of being bad." Essentially, the problem of the individual who would win in life is to want genuine goodness more than his sins. It is a strange, sad dilemma a man finds himself in, to sin yet hate his sin, to want goodness yet to want sinfulness more. The crux of the matter is to bring oneself to the point of wanting to be healed like the man at Bethesda; then that power over your lower nature will be permanently obtained. When you honestly make the break with sin and want moral power more, God will give it to you.

The classic illustration of this truth, of course, is

the famous experience of Saint Augustine. He was a brilliant youth, immersed in the sinfulness of the pagan Roman world in which he lived. Yet he aspired to spiritual power. He felt the instinct of creativeness within him, urging him to higher levels of life. But despite the many areas of his life which he cleansed, sin held him in the form of one particularly strong offense. He hated this sin, yet loved it more. One day he cried out, "O Lord, free me from my sins," but added as in a parenthesis, "all save one." God answered the parenthesis, for obviously the parenthesis was the prayer. The deepest desire is inevitably the true prayer. Again he prayed to God, saying, "O Lord, free me from my sins," but again added parenthetically, "all save one," and once more God answered the parenthesis, for it was still the prayer. Augustine was too real and strong a man to be caught forever in this impasse. Accordingly, one day he prayed, "Lord, free me from my sins," and by a herculean effort of will and desire and in agony of spirit added, desperately, "I mean *all* my sins—every one of them, even the sin of the parenthesis." In that instant the great thing happened. His chains fell clanking and broken from him. He was a free man. Subsequently he became one of the noblest figures in the long and honored history of the Christian Church.

You too can be free from your sin. Wouldn't you give a great deal for the exquisite feeling of freedom that would bring to you? Can you imagine the peace you would have in your heart to know that the temptation or desire or actual sin you have struggled with so long was at long last gone forever? You can have this great thing happen to you. Augustine's experience took place long ago, but it is being repeated to my knowledge again and again in the lives of modern men and women. Sin is an ancient but also a very modern phenomenon. It is one thing that does not change. Dr. Charles E. Jefferson was a minister for over a quarter of a century on Broadway in a time of vast change. Senator William E. Borah is reported to have said that in those twenty-five years more changes took place in our nation than in the preceding two hundred and fifty years. At the conclusion of his ministry, Doctor Jefferson said one of the things that had not changed was sin. It may be committed in different, even sophisticated form, but the thing is the same regardless of the form. One can, for example, get just as drunk and be just as contemptible and disgusting in an exotic, chromium-plated cocktail lounge with a woman as his companion as in the old-style sawdust-floored saloon with a bar-fly to keep him company.

But if sin is the same as in Augustine's day, so is the antidote unchanged. The same medicine can cure the same old disease. No matter what one's sin is, a sincere desire to be freed from it, plus an unquestioning faith in Christ, and the sin is conquered. I am using, as you will note, the word "sin" freely, and with no attempt to employ a more up-to-date synonym. There has been too soft an attitude with regard to the word, perhaps for fear it will sound like tabernacle evangelistic lingo, but why dodge the word? It is a good, strong English word and it means exactly what it says. Perhaps people have not wanted to hear much about sin. It is unpleasant and challenges us to moral effort, and our generation does not like effort. Like every disease, however, he is a wise man who will look straight at it, see it for what it is, and determine to end its unpleasantness not by blinding himself to it, but by coming to grips with it and ridding himself of

it. If you need a physical operation, you will face it
and have it performed, to the end that your body may
enjoy health. By the same token, if you need a moral
operation, face it and have it performed, that your
soul and mind and body may enjoy health.

What the old theologians called sin is still destruc-
tively active and its processes are subtle. A sin is like
a wound; indeed, it is a wound in the mind. Sorrow
is a wound also, but it is a clean wound. It hurts
terribly and may pain for an extended period, but it
heals because it is a clean wound and the healthy tissue of one's life draws about it. Sin, on the contrary,
being unclean, does not heal but continues to dissem-
inate poison throughout the personality. This poison
manifests itself in jumpy nerves, vague feelings that
things are wrong, or that something sinister is going
to happen. Even if it be deeply submerged in the
mind until one thinks he has forgotten it, the rotting
process continues, and from this seat of infection ill
health is produced in the personality. Oftentimes the
physical well-being is disturbed. People in the
strength of youth may carry their sin because of the
sheer vigor of their young lives. But when middle
age comes and the natural vigor tends to abate, the
resistance is weakened and many a man goes to pieces.
The number of men breaking down today from afflic-
tions related to the heart and nervous system is alarm-
ing. Most of these breakdowns are ascribed to over-
work or worry, and undoubtedly in many cases this
is a true diagnosis, but it must also be said that in
many cases the original or, at least, contributory cause
is a sin committed perhaps long ago which was never
exorcised or cleaned out from the consciousness by
a spiritual operation. You can win when you let the

Great Physician get that rotting moral tissue out of your life.

The way in which faith in God through surrender to Christ is effective in solving this troublesome problem was illustrated in a letter I received some time ago. It came from a young professor of science in a certain university. He said he listened to a radio talk in which I made statements similar to those you have just read. He had for a long time been in a conflict between a desire to live a good, clean life and the pull of a particular sin. He admitted that while he had prayed for freedom from this sin, that in his heart he had never really meant it, and, in fact, confessed that sometimes while in prayer the enticement of his sin tormented his mind. It was the old story of Plato's man who rides two horses, a black one and a white. He hated his sin but he loved it more. On the strength of the unequivocal promise made in the radio talk he said he went to his room and like a man bent on doing something desperate knelt and strongly told God he meant what he was going to ask. He was wise enough evidently to tell the Lord that if his mind attempted that old trick of the human mind universal, of disputing what his lips said, to disregard the mind and believe only what his words indicated. He reminded God that he understood the deeper desires of this man who was praying, the dilemma he was in, the ebb and flow of good and evil in his life and asked the Lord to take what he said at face value no matter what his subconscious mind thought about and itself tried to say while his conscious mind was speaking by word of mouth. For the first time he was utterly sincere and he informed me that there came over him a great elation, for he knew that something had snapped within him. He knew he had the victory at last. He could, he declared, have shouted, in the words of Saint Paul, "I can do all things"—even this—"through Christ who has given me the strength." This letter came to me about six months after this incident occurred. He said he wanted to be sure about the experience before writing it. That was the scientist speaking and it added force to his concluding words: "I am happy to report that the experience grows ever more real. Power deepens as I keep myself close to Christ. I am through with the old sin. It works as you said it would."

In every problem you can move up to a better life, one filled with spiritual power, and extract the real joy from living if you want it enough to take the freedom and strength which Christ so freely offers. To persuade the human spirit to accept freedom is, strangely enough, a very great difficulty. We come to the very door of freedom with the glorious land of peace, happiness, and success lying beyond, ours for the taking. But after a longing look in its direction with a sigh we turn back to our prisons. Dr. Smiley Blanton, the eminent New York psychiatrist who gives his clinical time to our consultation work at the Marble Church, has worked out the formula of this process which he has observed so often in his long experience in counseling. First is conviction of sin, then confession. This is followed by restitution and absolution. The next step is freedom, but the tragedy is that instead of proceeding further and taking freedom, many people go back over the circle again and still again. Apparently, they can never quite bring themselves to believe freedom is theirs or, believing it, to take this benefit that God in his goodness offers them. When, by an act of real faith, they do break the circle, then the great thing happens which we call conversion.

Life becomes new and fresh. Then they know of a
truth we are right when we say, "You Can Win."

The great preacher of yesterday, Dwight L. Moody,
was the speaker some years ago at a meeting of several
thousand prisoners in a certain state penitentiary. It
had been announced that after Mr. Moody's address
a pardon would be announced by the governor, who
would present this pardon to a prisoner of good record.
No one but the governor knew who the fortunate prisoner was to be. There was naturally great excitement
and expectancy and not a few hearts beat high with
hope. Finally, the great moment came and the governor stepped forward with the pardon in his hand.
He read out a name, "John Smith" (that is not his
real name). There was a wave of applause but no one
came forward. The governor called the name a second time, but still the prisoner, Smith, did not move
from his seat, held fast doubtless by his disbelief that
he, a life-termer, should be granted freedom. Finally,
near-by companions pushed him from his seat and
Smith came forward with tears streaming down his
cheeks to take the pardon from the hand of the governor. Then the warden commanded the great audi-
ence of prisoners to fall in and march back to their cells.
When his cell-mates came marching past him, Smith,
still holding the pardon, fell in, and, taking up the
lockstep, started the old march back to his long-es-
tablished place behind the bars. It became necessary
for the attendants to pull him from the line saying,
"Man, don't you know you are free?"

So Christ comes to us with the glorious statement,
"He hath sent me to preach deliverance to the captives," and that is just what many of us are, prisoners
of the senses, prisoners of our fears, captives of our
sins, but offered freedom, we march back to the same

old things that hold us fast. But Christ says to us, "You can be free if you want to be." If you will just tell him you want a better life and mean it, he will give it to you; and when you get it, you will wonder how you ever lived without it. So Christ offers you freedom. Take it and don't march back to prison. God and you are unconquerable.

CHAPTER V

DON'T BE A VICTIM OF THE OBSTACLE COMPLEX

ONE of the most widely used words in America today is the word "complex." Succinctly stated, a complex may be defined as a system of emotionally toned ideas ranged around one central idea. The most commonly discussed complex is the inferiority complex, in which the central idea is disbelief in oneself growing out of a feeling of inadequacy.

By the obstacle complex we mean the notion that insurmountable difficulties stand in the way of one's success and happiness. It is the unhappy influence of the fixed idea that one "cannot." It is the "I can't" philosophy become dominant in one's personality and life. Again and again in talking with people the obstacle complex arises. "Why not try this?" we advise. "Or why not do this?" we suggest. "Oh, I can't," is the answer. "That would not work," is the excuse. One cites example after example of people who have achieved in the face of similar difficulties from beginnings just as unpromising. The rejoinder usually is, "Well, it may have been so in their case, but my situation is different." The victim of the obstacle complex seems to entertain the notion that his obstacle has something unique about it, something that no one ever experienced before.

For a perfect example of the obstacle complex and its working let us turn again to the greatest book on psychology ever written, the Holy Bible. There we read the familiar story of the children of Israel, who were making their way out of captivity in Egypt to the Promised Land, where they were to be happy, free from oppression, and where every man would have the opportunity for a successful life. As they approached the Promised Land spies were sent out to bring back a description of the country and the inhabitants. The leaders wanted to know what opposition they might expect. The spies returned with the report that it was indeed a land flowing with milk and honey. To verify their opinion of the fertility of the land they brought back a cluster of grapes so large it required two men to carry it suspended on a pole between their shoulders. But they were very pessimistic about their ability to take the country, for, they said, "We found giants in the land"—great, huge fellows. And they added this striking sentence, "And we were in our own sight as grasshoppers, and so we were in their sight." In this incident we have an obstacle complex splendidly delineated. It is a modern problem described in an ancient book. Undoubtedly, there are many people who say every day in effect, "And we were in our own sight as grasshoppers, and so we were in their sight." They are victims of the obstacle complex.

Let us examine this story from the Bible, which teaches such good psychology, and see what it tells us about overcoming the obstacle complex. God, it seemed, had prepared for these people a land flowing with milk and honey. They had been in suffering and privation but now were marching under God's leadership away from all that to a glorious country of prosperity. In similar fashion God comes to us in some Egypt of the spirit and points us to a land of promise. To every individual reading this book I can with assurance say that God in his goodness has prepared for you somewhere and in some way a great and wonderful life, and it is for you to find it and to take it. God lays up stores of gold and precious jewels in the earth, but men have to find them and mine them for their own use. So God has for you a life of happiness and well-being, but you, through faith in him and by means of industry in yourself, must discover it and win it for yourself.

I have a friend who, before the beginning of the depression about nine years ago, had a position which paid him something like eight thousand dollars a year. During those halcyon days when he had more money than he needed and when the spirit of speculation was much in the air, he bought a little rocky farm. He knew absolutely nothing about farming but liked the quaint appearance of the old-fashioned farmhouse. As the depression proceeded, he finally lost his position and after some months his reserve was dissipated and he was down to hard scratching. At this juncture it became necessary, due to lack of funds, to move into the farmhouse which he had purchased just as a place to go on Saturday afternoons. He tried to till the soil, but his inexperience and the paucity of the ground made that attempt unsuccessful. Finally he confided to me that was going into the chicken business. I asked him what he knew about chickens and he replied that the only thing he knew about them was that they came from eggs. However, he had the will to learn and was not afraid to work, and he persevered, with the result that today he is a successful chicken farmer, making an adequate living, and is happier than he has ever been in all his life. If at the bottom of his depression, his Egypt, I should have told him that one day he would be a successful chicken farmer, he would have ridiculed me. God had prepared for him, you see, a land flowing with milk and honey. The Promised Land in his case, as in your case, may not be what you want or expect, but it is a good land, nevertheless. By prayer and a desire to do God's will you can find it. This land flowing with milk and honey is not only a Bible story. It is an actual fact for every individual.

I can well imagine that many people who read these words may experience genuine difficulty in seeing in their situation any evidence of a land flowing with milk and honey. Recently, as I was thinking about this chapter, I was riding in a New York subway. Across from me I noticed a man and woman sitting very still and quiet, not speaking but both staring straight ahead. Their dress indicated that frugality born of financial adversity. But some trouble worse than lack of money must have fallen upon them. His face was drawn and white. A deep hurt showed in his eyes. Her eyes were red from weeping. A tear coursed slowly down her cheek. After a while I saw his hand steal surreptitiously for hers beside him on the seat. I could but dimly imagine what tragedy had come to this couple who, for a few flashing subway stations, touched the edge of my life. Willa Cather says there are only two or three human stories. But whatever it was, and it had to be one of the many old human sorrows common to all men, the fact is that somewhere beyond even their Egypt of the spirit, if they only knew it, lies the fair country which God always prepares for his children. The reason trouble and tragedy and failure defeat us is because we will not sturdily assume the fact of a profound good and diligently seek to find it.

I used to know a man in a city in upstate New York who had been for forty years the weather man. He

had become so identified with the weather that he
acted almost as though it was his weather. He was
very sensitive about it. When I first knew him, I
tried to jolly him a little about the weather. I found
out soon that he did not like that very well; it was a
reflection on his weather. He had observed the weather
for so long that he had become a sort of philosopher.
One day he said to me, "I have been charting the
weather for forty years and have discovered one thing,
that there are about as many clear, sunshiny days as
there are cloudy and rainy ones." Do you see what
that means? It means that life is scrupulously fair—
that the rain signifies one great fact—sunshine will
follow.

I have always found inspiration and understanding
in the story of a girl from a Middle-Western town who
came to New York where every prospect promised a
brilliant career. She met and fell in love with a fine
young man of corresponding capabilities. Then the
blow fell. Her mother suffered a paralytic stroke and
was rendered practically helpless. The issue was clear
cut. The daughter must return to the little town and
care for her mother or provide outside help for that
purpose. She decided on the former and, with the
visions of her career falling around her, came back to
the small town to what, in her disappointment, she
felt would be a dull and mediocre life. As time passed,
her engagement was also broken because she felt she
could not leave her invalid mother. She became a
teacher in the public schools though the task seemed
prosaic and uninspiring. One day a bright-eyed lad
asked her for advice about his lifework. Should he
go further and have a college education? She inspired
him by picturing what he could make of his life. Perhaps she infused him with some of the glow she once

felt about her own broken career. Inspiring youth became a passion with her. Seeing a girl with musical
ability, she whispered dreams into her soul. Seeing a
boy with gifts of speech, she held before him pictures
of great audiences listening to his words. Seeing a boy
with mechanical genius, she beguiled him with visions
of high achievement. She fired them all with the glory
of human service. She helped them see life's heights
and far horizons. So they began to go out of that
little town, going to college and then to the ends of
the earth—preachers, missionaries, musicians, states-
men, physicians, all of them the spiritual children of
a woman now growing gray, who once thought life
had fallen in upon her but now beloved by a host, to
each of whom she had given a wisp of her own unful-
filled dream. In her dismal Egypt, all the time a
promised land lay waiting for her—the true, noble
career which God in his strange way of providence had
prepared for her.

Another thing we read in this story is that there are
obstacles in the way of reaching the land flowing with
milk and honey. These spies who went out said that
there were giants in the land, standing in the way of
their possession of the country. Truly they do look
like giants. The Promised Land is never attained
cheaply. I remember hearing a boy who had a minor
position in a store say that the boss, to use his words,
"was sitting in clover." That might have been im-
pressive to some, but I knew the boss. I knew that the
boss was in the office long after the boy and all the
other employees had gone home at night. I knew the
boss had his home mortgaged to the hilt for the benefit of his business. I knew the boss was carrying on his
payrolls and on his heart employees whom he could
not afford to keep but whom he would not throw upon

the harsh mercy of life. The boss had built a great store and attained a land flowing with milk and honey, but he had to work for it. He had to overcome his giants.

There are two things we ought to realize about a giant: first, that most of him is bluff. It is rewarding sometimes to turn to a dictionary for a definition of common words. It clears up many a misunderstanding. As I was developing this chapter I turned to the dictionary for the definition of the word "giant," and this is what I read—"an imaginary being of great size." Note the important word in that definition. After all, a giant, including the giant obstacle that keeps you from the Promised Land of prosperity and happiness, is most of him imaginary, as our dictionary definition indicates. Take a good honest look at your chief difficulty and see if much of it is not weak and harmless.

Walking down Broadway in New York recently, I noticed an enormous figure striding toward me. He was at least fifteen feet tall and bedecked with advertisements of a clothing store. He was the best-made giant I ever saw, walking with mechanical perfection and awing the throngs among whom he moved as a colossus. Upon a close scrutiny, however, I saw the deception, for he was in reality only a little fellow, five feet high, atop stilts. Ten feet of him were false. It is entirely possible that the giants that move against you may be of a comparable proportion of imagination. This fact does not overlook the reality of the substantial part of your giant, but if you see him for the size he actually is, you will see yourself for the size you actually are and know in your heart that you are well able to meet and deal with that giant.

We seem to have an eye only for the difficulties and

fail to see the possibilities of success. Listen in to the average conversation. We talk of world peace, and at once the barriers in the way of that ideal are advanced. We discuss the return of business prosperity, and instantly the tenor of our conversation is pessimistic. We consider our own individual affairs, and begin to enumerate the reasons why we cannot do a thing. Our pictures are for the most part negative and as a result our achievements are negative. We give the impression of men who are with puny hands feebly trying to hold back a great sea that is about to break over us.

It calls to mind many summers by the sea. How does a good swimmer or surf-bather deal with a vast wave about to break? Does he allow it to crash down upon him? Not at all. He leaps headlong into it and in a moment his sharp, clean strokes have brought him beyond the wave into calm water, while the mass of water crashes in harmless foam upon the shore. The swimmer is not paralyzed by a picture of disaster but masters the overwhelming weight and power of the water by a picture of his ability to conquer the wave by his own buoyancy and skill and nerve.

A mental picture of oneself drawn in highlights is very likely to result in success while one drawn in somber color is pointed toward failure. Henry Thoreau, out of wise reflection by Walden Pond, tells us, "What a man thinks of himself, that it is which determines, or rather indicates, his fate." The Bible says of man—"As he thinketh in his heart, so is he." All of which leads us to the conclusion that we are what we picture ourselves to be.

Go up against your giant with a realization of the bully and, therefore, coward he is. Perhaps your giant is composed largely of the vacuous components of fear, worry, and imaginings. All of them are naturally disturbing, but in reality they are ghosts and phantoms. It is a tragedy to be defeated by shadows which courage and high-hearted attack could soon dissipate.

The man with the obstacle complex, who can see only the size of the giants in his path, is defeated before he starts. But the man who says, "This difficulty is not as bad as it looks," and forthwith goes to work with what he has, is the man who wins in this life. A friend of mine graduated from college but could not get a job because of the depression. Many people can testify what a giant that experience is. I used the wrong word—what he wanted was a position, but he finally took a job, and the best one he could get was selling cakes and buns from a little pushcart in the financial district of New York. It was not much of a job for a college man, but he set himself to make it a real job. He found presently a poor woman who had a marvelous culinary gift, and he arranged with her to make his cakes and buns. His sales at once increased and he began to see visions around his pushcart which today are realized in a fine, large, successful bakery, employing a large number of people. This happened, mind you, between 1929 and 1938 when giants were walking all over America, frightening people into accepting defeat without a struggle.

Another thing to realize about a giant is that there is always a way of getting around him. He is awkward and clumsy. He cannot defeat you if you are alert and determined. I know one may say: "I'd like to see you get around my giant. My situation is different. Other people may have hope, but not I; there are too many factors against me." Now, my friend, do not get to enumerating those factors, for, if you do, we will simply get lost in endless detail. Let's keep the proposition simple. I say if you look straight at your difficulty,

optimistically and with the obstacle complex elim-
inated from your mind, there is a way around it. You
may seem like a prisoner in a closed room, no doors,
no windows, no openings. No chance to escape is
evident, but if you will diligently search that closed
room, you will find a secret button. Press it and you
are free. Your situation may be unpromising to your
obstacle blinded view, but the button is there nevertheless. Bacon agrees with this truth: "If a man look
sharply and attentively, he shall see fortune, for though
she is blind, she is not invisible." I do not say you can
vanquish or remove all obstacles, but you can get
around them and win the victory by a flank movement
if not a frontal attack. Get the attitude—There is
always some way around this difficulty. Then sit down
and study it with faith in your point of view. You
shake your head? You know better from long, sad
experience? Well, consider this bit of life history. It
is a story by Channing Pollock and is good medicine
for the victim of the obstacle complex.[1]

"A year ago I lectured in Brigham Young University
at Provo, Utah," said Mr. Pollock. "I had been travel-
ing hard, speaking once or twice every day, was very
tired, and felt very sorry for myself. After the lecture
a man, standing among several who had come onto the
platform, said something kind about my talk. I turned
to shake his hand and found that he had no hands.
Then I looked up to meet his eye and found that he
had no eyes.

"Next morning my friend telephoned me and said,
'Let's take a drive and see Bear Canyon. It's lovely
at this time of year.' The idea of seeing the Canyon
with a man who couldn't see interested me. But perhaps no one else ever saw that Canyon as clearly and

---

[1] Reprinted by permission of the author.

appreciatively as my blind companion. He kept point-
ing this way and that. 'Look at the crag,' he exclaimed,
'with the shadows slipping away from it! Look at the
colors in that valley!'

" 'How long since you really saw them last,' I inquired at length.

" 'More than thirty years,' my friend answered, 'but
I know every rock and tree. When I'm depressed, I
always come here to look at them. I can't tell you
what those mountains mean to me!'

"This man, a kinsman of Abraham Lincoln's mother,
Nancy Hanks, was blinded and crippled in a mine
explosion when he was twenty-one. After that he
earned ten thousand dollars to pay for his education at
Leland Stanford, Columbia, and Harvard. He has
delivered over six thousand lectures and unaccom-
panied has crossed the continent fifty-five times. He
can't even read raised type with his fingers, because he
has no fingers. But he has memorized over forty
thousand words of classical literature, so that he can
repeat them to himself when he wants to read. He
keeps house alone in a lovely cottage, doing his cook-
ing with a wooden hand he had made, and he goes
fishing, using another kind of artificial hand. I'm
going to spend a week with my friend in that little
house some day; he is one of the busiest, happiest,
and most companionable persons I ever met. I had a letter from him a few weeks ago. He wrote, 'The mountains are so beautiful in their new blanket of snow.' "

Here is another point we ought to remember. These
spies said when they looked at the giants, "We were
in our own sight as grasshoppers, and," they added
ruefully, "so were we in their sight." Of course they
were. The world is likely to think no higher of you
than in your heart you think of yourself. If you think

of your obstacles as giants and dwell upon the difficulties which are in your way, and are constantly harping upon the tremendous problems which face you, naturally you will cause them to grow to proportions that are totally unwarranted, and as you allow them to grow, you yourself will become smaller and more impotent. As you face your giant, see him as he really is, and when you see him as he really is, you will see yourself as you really are. Think your giant down and think yourself up.

Now, see what follows: Two of the spies said they could go over and conquer this country. They had no obstacle complex. They were strong, dominant men, the kind of men who win over anything. Where did they get this spirit? The answer is, they felt that God was with them. They had an overwhelming sense that God was by their side. They had heard him say, "Fear not, I am with you." How could they be defeated when they had God with them? So they threw back their shoulders and their eyes flashed, and they radiated power. Then there came a day when they finally persuaded the children of Israel that they could win, and they came up, ready to go into the Promised Land. Joshua cried out, "Tomorrow will the Lord do wonders among you." He admonished them to be strong and of good courage. Now something interesting happened. We read in the story this significant fact: "Now the Amorites'—that is, the giants'—hearts melted." "Melted" is a good word. It means that their hearts simply went to pieces. "Neither was there any spirit in them." In other words, the giants were punctured and they shriveled up to their real size. Now these people who had previously felt insignificant became the real giants. When the giants stood in the presence of people who had the absolute conviction that they were invincible, a conviction which came to them because they believed that God was with them, the giants lost their power. So will your giants lose their power. Don't allow yourself to think that you are defeated by anything. You are never defeated until you think you are. There is a land flowing with milk and honey waiting for you. Go and get it. You will never get it, however, if you go after it in your own strength, because you are not strong enough, but if you take God with you, you will become so strong that no obstacle or difficulty can defeat you.

I am glad to count among my friends one of the outstanding woman executives of this country, the head of a great commercial organization. After years of experience in dealing with people and having brought herself up from the lowest rung of the ladder, she made this fine statement, which every one of us should remember: "You can fear yourself to failure or you can fire yourself to success." She is one person who has learned the secret of absolute conquest of the inferiority complex. I asked her once to explain the secret of her phenomenal success, and she replied, "If I have been able to make anything of myself and overcome my obstacles, it has been due to a text from the Bible." Here is the text which this great business woman said was the source of her power, "If God be for us, who can be against us?" She found the secret discovered by the fortunate ones, that in religious faith—and by that I mean real faith, not formal observance—the sense of inferiority shrivels up as a moth in a flame. When one gets the knowledge that God is with him, guiding and directing him, he becomes aware of an inward strength and power that nothing in the world can defeat.

I can almost hear some of my readers saying: "That sounds very well, but I never saw anything like that in religion. Religion only means going to church and listening to a sermon." Well, my friend, you have stated and answered your own failure. If religion has been only form for you, it is nothing but form. But if you will really put your faith in God and trust your life to him, religion will change from form to power. People who trust God with unquestioning, childlike faith become undefeatable, indomitable persons who do things and for whom life is a never-ending delight. Shaw, in his play, *St. Joan,* has pictured this quality in the heroic maid of Orleans. She comes into the headquarters of the discouraged French general whose handful of men are opposed by an overwhelming force of English. Joan tells him not to be afraid of them, for he can defeat them. He is annoyed with such foolish bravado and sarcastically asks her how she proposes to defeat so superior an enemy. With a wonderful smile on her face, that glorious smile of certain victory over anything, even the impossible, she drew a flashing sword which sparkled in the sunlight. "With this sword," she said: "this is God's sword. He hid it for me behind the altar in the church of Saint Catherine. Nothing can stand in the way of God's sword." This faith made a simple country girl the immortal heroine of France. Take God's sword in your hand, my discouraged, defeated friend; take God's shining sword and leap up on the battlements of the hosts that encamp against you. With God's sword in your hand charge upon your enemies of fear and inferiority and disbelief in yourself. Charge like the famous Light Brigade against your weakness and your sins and your temptations. With God's sword in your hands they haven't a chance against you.

I would not presume to offer you this sort of advice unless I believed it and knew it to be true. It works, as I have myself discovered, and as I have seen others find it to do. One day into my study came a big, husky fellow who said he needed spiritual help. I asked him how he happened to come to our church that day. "About six weeks ago," he said, "I was riding down Fifth Avenue and as the bus passed this church I noticed the sign on your outdoor pulpit." This is a large bulletin board in front of the church on which we put sentences we hope will be helpful to passers-by. "What was on the sign?" I asked. He replied, "It said, 'You can succeed if you realize the power that is in you.' " "Yes," I said, "I remember that." "Well," he continued, "that struck me and I was a bit surprised too to think that the church was interested in helping people that way. So," he went on, "I started attending your church, and now I am coming for a personal conference because I have become persuaded that there is something practical in religion which can help me acquire the strength I need so badly. Tell me," he said, "how to get this benefit from religion." I replied: "It is very simple and not at all complicated —just dedicate your life to God and ask him to give you his help. But," I continued, "you must believe that God is helping you." I reminded him that the gospel does not tell us to try harder but to believe harder. We are not to struggle for God's power but to take his power which he freely offers. God's help is not an achievement but a gift. Have we not often noted the foolish mistake some people make? They have something in their life from which they wish to free themselves, and they heroically say, "I will defeat this." But even when they say that and mean it sincerely, it is a well-known psychological principle that the effect is to fix the thing more firmly in the consciousness. On the contrary, when one says, "God will do this for me," and really believes that he will, the thing is done. Faith is stronger than will. Well, to finish the story about this man. He said he would practice the advice given. I did not see him for several months, as he made a long business trip, but when he returned, he came in and said with a glad smile on his face, "It works." And so it will for you if you try it. Don't be a victim of the obstacle complex, but be a master in life. That's what religion is for. That's why you need religion.

CHAPTER VI

YOU HAVE IT IN YOU TO SUCCEED

"TO be or not to be?" This immortal soliloquy from Shakespeare's *Hamlet* is characterized by Professor William Lyon Phelps as the six greatest words outside of the Bible. They seem a bit out of style today, however, for many people are thinking gloomily in terms of a less classical but realistic couplet—

> "For of all the sad words of tongue or pen,
> The saddest are these: 'It might have been.'"

This might conceivably be termed "the might-have-been era." It is an easily explained situation. Contemporary conditions have so modified the plans, hopes, and ambitions of the average person that unless he has won a decided victory over his spirit, he may fall naturally into the habit of contemplating and dwelling upon what might have been rather than what may be.

"To be or not to be?"—that is the question faced not only by Hamlet but by thousands of discouraged Americans. We need a resurgence of that sturdy old American spirit of taking in the belt and with man-sized determination making something fine out of the most unlikely possibilities. Napoleon once roared: "Circumstances—what are circumstances? I make circumstances." And Disraeli said, "We are not creatures of circumstance; we are creators of circumstance." Of course, times are hard and the situation for many people is little short of tragic. But we are still alive and we have dear ones who love us. This is America and the

115

Stars and Stripes of Democracy still wave. The sun continues to shine. And, best of all, "God's in his heaven" even if all is not right with the world. As Tom Paine, in the dark days of the American Revolution, said, sturdily, "Let us thank God for this crisis, for it gives us opportunity to show that we are men."

I have always admired the story of a strong-minded mother in a poor cabin in the wilderness, who, on her deathbed, called to her side a gangling, lanky lad. Holding his hand and looking into his eyes, out of long years of indomitable ambition in the midst of crushing hardship, she said with intensity in her tone, "Abe, be somebody." I have little doubt that years later, when Lincoln became the Great Emancipator, he could hear the echo of those words of a pioneer mother, "Abe, be somebody." It is not representative of the truest nature of our American stock to weep long in the dark valley of "it might have been." We surely will respond to our pioneer, dauntless, courageous heritage which whispers, "Be somebody."

Say what you will, the thing that makes a real man is that quality or impulse within which makes him want to do the most with his life. When that impulse becomes weakened, regardless of what a man has attained, he is in decline; his day is done. To take life in his two strong hands, to apply to it the power of his brain and brawn, and out of his effort achieve something honorable and worth while is the process out of which real men are made. To make yourself a real man and stay that way until life ends, through both adversity and prosperity, is one of the few supreme achievements of this life. Some men whimper and become weak under adversity. Some men become soft and weak under prosperity. Both types are failures. To grow strong and retain that quality until you step into the valley of the shadow is to succeed in life. Even in hard times like the present some men are steadily forging ahead while their contemporaries sit complaining about lack of opportunity. The ultimate test of life is not what we attain in possessions or position, but the quality of spirit with which we meet whatever comes.

A friend of mine, a student of the world famous psychologist, Dr. Sigmund Freud, called on his old teacher in Vienna just prior to the unhappy cricumstances which forced Freud to leave his homeland, a victim of the Nazi terror. As they parted, conscious of impending adversity, the student repeated to the old scholar those magnificent words of Horace, "Though the great world be overthrown, let us still be undismayed." Freud's face lighted up as he acknowledged the comfort and courage he had derived from that philosophy through his long life of conflict and trouble.

Fine as that is, however, there is something better. It is not alone to be passively undismayed by the outrageous slings of fortune, but to move against your troubles with the determination to win. So many people have suffered reversals and losses as they have attempted to realize their ambitions and reach their goals that discouragement hangs like a pall over the land. With it has come a rather widespread sense of futility. "What's the use?" is a question all too generally heard. Men consider sadly what they dreamed of being, what they hoped to do. For many the contrast between their anticipation and the present realization is deeply disappointing.

But some men do not let it break their spirit. They know they have it in them to succeed. Here is a man who has worked for years to build a business. He has put his strength of mind and nerve into its development. It has been an honest American business, helpful to the community and to his employees. Because some unsocial business leaders have violated ethical and humanitarian principles, this man and thousands of men like him suffer the sting of criticism for acts for which they were in no sense responsible. It is no more fair that all business should be condemned because some leaders are dishonest or unsocial than that all labor should be castigated because some leaders are dishonest or communistic.

Not only does this man of business suffer demagogic criticism, but in addition the possibility of failure ever stares him in the face. The fate of employees, for whom he feels a sense of responsibility, adds to the strain upon him. He sees all that he has scarified and worked for through the years threaten to go down in social and financial storms to the origin of which he contributed no more than any of us who have lived in this country in the last fifty years. To him should be said that, despite all difficulties, he has it in him to succeed as he has always wanted to succeed. He can still round out the dreamed of patterns of his life.

Here is a man who has never been able to get ahead financially. He has always been just a few dollars above the bottom of his bank account. Many times, in fact, the bottom shows through. Rent and clothes and the secondhand car and insurance and the children's education constitute a never-ending struggle and anxiety. Once as a lad he dreamed long dreams, but life has given him more drudgery than romance. He is heroic, nevertheless, and men like him make you realize how many "real" folk there are in the world. I met one of these men on the street in New York recently. What a dreamer he was as a boy! He is a salesman now, on a small salary. His suit, neatly pressed, was shiny. The straw hat, which he removed to mop his brow, was at least a three-year-old, and the head he revealed was becoming a bit bald on top. But on his face was the old cheery smile and the old light in his eye was undimmed. He voiced faith in his country, talked affectionately of his church, where he is an active worker, and said he was sure better days were ahead for us all. He would have laughed at the thoughts going through my mind. His shiny suit became for me a shining suit of armor; his old hat, a gleaming helmet, and he was astride a white horse like a champion of the old days of chivalry, waging a noble fight for his fair lady. I must confess I left him with eyes a little misty, but heart-stirred by the inspiration of a real man, who had not lost the glory of life even in hardship. I wondered if perhaps he did not have to come to grips with discouragement many a time during these days, when selling is pretty hard work. Did he not, I wondered, have a battle of the spirit to fight not a few nights as he lay sleepless, staring into the dark? To him let it be said that he too has it in him to succeed as he has always dreamed of succeeding. He is a pretty noble figure as he is, but with character like that he can go on to better things. Any man of average ability can succeed if he makes up his mind to and keeps it made up long enough. William Jennings Bryan said, "Destiny is not a matter of chance. It is a matter of choice."

There are many types of people I am thinking of in this chapter—the man, for example, who is a champion of ideals, a crusader for the good. There are men and women who dedicate their lives to the making of a better world. They labor for the spread of good will and righteousness in the earth. They work for social justice, for improved conditions for the vast number of underprivileged people. They earnestly desire these advances in human welfare to be achieved in substantial and permanent form.

There too are the seekers after peace among the nations, the builders of world courts and leagues of nations, who by every means attempt to create in men's hearts that sort of spirit which will end war.

There too are the preachers and religious teachers who see the gospel, for which they give their lives, watered down or cast aside by a crass, vulgar paganism, both in and out of the church. Evil is rampant and the followers of Christ seem, as in New Testament times, such a "little flock."

All of these high-minded people, whose labors seem at times so hopeless, against whom the odds are so heavy, need to be reminded—"You can succeed." Do not allow yourself to become cynical or permit your enthusiasm to be tarnished by the acid of futility.

Carry on. It is the noblest thing of all to fight for a good cause. Evil may win many a skirmish, conquer in many a battle, but at the end of the campaign good will win. "In the long run," says Froude, the historian, "it is well with the good and ill with the bad." This world is somehow built on moral foundations. This, he points out, is the one lesson history teaches. Suppose Christianity is diluted by many with cheap and tawdry compromise. Suppose the world in the form of profanity, drunkenness, and immorality has made terrific inroads among those who once themselves, or whose forebears, were honorable men and women of God. Regrettable as it is, it has been so before. Culture has waned at other periods in history and the vulgar cult has gained the ascendancy. But always—remember this—always a purified Church has at length purified the world. The good never loses.

To the person of thirty and forty years or there-abouts let it be said, You have it in you to succeed. Many of you are feeling the pinch of the growing discrimination against your age group. It is based on a false philosophy that length of years determines quality of life.

A wise newspaper editorial said recently, "The function of science is not to add more years to life but to add more life to years." That is exactly the proposition with which Christianity is concerned. Christianity gives you the power to live while you live, regardless of how long or short your span of life may be. There is much discussion today as to when one begins to live. The phrase, "Life begins at forty," seems to have found its way into our common speech and has become a sort of axiom. This is an important question, for out of every one thousand people in America two hundred and sixty are forty or over. Statisticians estimate that by 1960 this will have risen to three hundred and sixty out of every one thousand. We are becoming a nation of elders due to declining infant mortality, longer expectancy and the improvement of public health. The problem of the individual over forty has become increasingly important in view of today's unemployment. A distinguished physician says our age has acquired what he describes as "forty-phobia." When you have "forty-phobia," you have the mistaken notion that the ability of a man over forty is limited, that physically as well as mentally he has begun to atrophy.

No more false philosophy was ever developed in this nation than the idea that the individual over forty is in any way incompetent. As a matter of fact, every evidence indicates that during that period a person is just coming to the height of his powers. It is highly signifi-cant that nearly every political, industrial, and professional leader in this country is today forty or above. The Koreans have a pleasing philosophy. They say that every person is recreated at sixty and begins a new cycle of life. That is the Korean way of saying that life begins at sixty.

This problem of when life begins, however, is not related solely to our work. Many people in America who have satisfactory positions are still concerned with the question as to when one begins to live. Many people of forty or thereabouts find themselves in a position of crisis. It is a period of life when dreams tend to fade into hard realism. In youth one has optimistic hopes of the future. Life is an adventure. Great things lie ahead. There comes a day, however, when many disappointments may become disillusionment. The dream fades like sunlight obscured by a passing cloud, leaving the pathway of life, hitherto bright and sparkling, now gray and disconsolate. The final pattern of one's life now seems fairly discernible. The mystery, and with it much of the romance, accordingly, is dissipated. One acquires the feeling that there is nothing to look forward to. Nothing is sadder than the aging of a person's spirit and the tragedy is that it happens regardless of years. Some people are old at thirty, others are youthful at ninety. Age is not determined by the calendar or the birth certificate, but by the inner spirit. Today multitudes of people are asking, "Does life begin at forty, or fifty, or at some other arbitrary period?" The answer is that one's age has nothing to do with the secret of life. Life begins the moment one opens his soul and mind to spiritual power. That is why the Man who knew more about human life than any other who ever lived said, "I am come that they might have life, and that they might have it more abundantly." That is, life begins and in an abundant manner when one becomes truly spiritual in his attitudes and motives. Life to be renewed requires an alchemy more skillful than materialistic or sensory methods can produce.

To young people I want to say—You have it in you to succeed despite the apparently unfavorable situation into which your advancing maturity has brought you. It may be difficult to secure the sort of opening you want or to which you feel you have a right. It may even be seemingly next to impossible to get a job. We extend not the hand of soft sympathy, for you do not want that. We extend the hand of a friend and say it is a hard world, but get your mind off that fact and fasten it to the truth, that despite all obstacles you can win. Consider this fact. Some members of your generation are going to win success. Why not you? Some will be the leaders in state, in business, in education, in the arts and sciences. Why not you? If you may be inclined to advance the argument that your obstacles are more difficult than those of many of your contemporaries, I suggest that twenty years from now you pick the leaders, read their life stories, and compare the status of their prospects in 1938 with your own at that date. Your chances at this moment are just as good as theirs. Do not give any credence whatever to that cynical complaint of the perennial failure, that America is no longer a land of opportunity. The man who has something in him can make a success of his life here, even now, as real men always have, and far better than in certain sections of the world which that same malcontent would have you believe are modern Utopias. A genuine American knows a man can go on to better things from situations totally unpromising because it has been done in this land no end of times. It is being done today. He does violence to the spirit of America as well as to the plain truth who would have us believe a man can no longer improve his lot in this country. Real men still find this American climate propitious for growth. Tuck the intrepid motto of Tennyson's "Ulysses" up against your heart and go ahead, "To strive, to seek, to find, and not to yield."

Recently I sat in the motor car of a friend of mine, a highly successful executive. As we rode along in the splendid chauffeur-driven automobile, my host's life story, which I knew well, again impressed me. The son of a good but poor family, he never had the benefit of an education, but by dint of hard work, clean living, and a desire to make something of his life, he came finally to a material and also character success. After leaving me that day he was going to call on a young man who operates a little ice-cream-cone stand at a summer resort. My friend some years ago assumed the responsibility for the education of this boy, who is now a senior in college. Laughingly he said it was not costing him much now, as the boy was always earning money for himself, as witness the ice-cream cones. It occurred to me to wonder, as the man drove on to see his young protégé, whether he had not given the boy something better than money—namely, a fine, manly spirit of self-reliance and strength of character.

The principal ingredients in successful living are courage of the come-what-may variety and the capacity for hard work. Very few people who attain success are deserving of the title, "genius." Theodore Roosevelt once declared he was just an ordinary fellow, but, "By George," he said, "I work at it more than most ordinary men." Of course he was more than an ordinary man, but without his intense driving power even he would not have been the great and dynamic "T. R."

You have it in you to succeed. Continuous hard

work, unremitting devotion to your job, be it large or small, important or insignificant, will bring success to you. Most people fail, not for lack of ability, but for lack of stamina. They simply won't work hard enough and long enough. The key to success consists of the willingness to work and work hard. Abraham Lincoln was once asked the secret of his success, and he replied that it consisted of three things: (1) work, (2) work, and the (3), he said, was work. One recalls the oft-repeated formula of Edison, that genius is two per cent inspiration and ninety-eight per cent perspiration. The plain fact is that all the successful people I ever knew, without exception, were people who worked hard, everlastingly keeping at their job until they had it mastered, and then keeping at it so they could keep it mastered.

Work for them is not drudgery, however, but the delight of their lives. When you begin to work hard at a job on the theory that it is worth while, you will get deeply into it and will make it worth while by the sheer infection of your enthusiasm. Then the job becomes play because you love it and would rather do it than anything in the world. Men like that take a job that may look ordinary and unattractive and far below their abilities and pour it so full of meaning and possibility that they make it grow in dignity and worth.

When I say you have it in you to succeed, I have excellent authority to substantiate that judgment. The late Professor William James, one of our wisest Americans, once made this startling appraisal of you and me: "Compared to what we ought to be, we are only half awake. We are making use of only a small part of our physical and mental resources. Stating the thing broadly," he continued, "the individual lives far within his limits. He possesses powers of various sorts which he habitually fails to use."

What this distinguished thinker and student of men is saying is that we have it in us to succeed. The first step in the achievement of success is to realize the power that is in you. We are wonderfully endowed and equipped by the Creator with intellectual power, charm of personality, and all the qualities which make for effective living, if we will only learn to see them and bring them into play.

You can succeed even when life is hard and difficult. Have you ever noticed that when hardship comes to some people, they get scared and go stumbling blindly around in the dark? Some even lose their way and go to pieces. Other folk, on the contrary, take hard blows and suffer keenly, but they seem to grow bigger and stronger and, instead of trouble defeating them, it is but a source of new strength and power. Some people rise victoriously over the trouble and sorrow of life. What is their secret?

We must realize, first of all, that hardship has a place in the well-ordered scheme of things. It is probably well that the Creator arranged this universe without consulting us, for we would have made it too soft. In the Franconia Notch in the White Mountains of New Hampshire, high on the mountainside, is the Great Stone Face. This face was immortalized by Hawthorne in one of his famous stories. Daniel Webster once said about it, "Men hang out their signs indicative of their respective trades—shoemakers hang out a gigantic shoe; jewelers, a monstrous watch; and the dentist hangs out a gold tooth; but up in the mountains of New Hampshire God Almighty has hung out a sign to show that there he makes men."

That is what this world is for—to make men, real men, and you cannot make men except by a process of fire and pain. The trees from which the wood of most exquisite grain is taken, that used in the finest furniture, come not from the valleys and sheltered places, but from the mountain tops, where, battling with the elements, struggling with the storms, fighting with the hurricane, they grow a fiber strong and clean. Frank Harris, a distinguished English writer, said: "Strong men are made by opposition like kites that go up against the wind." Hardship is hard to bear, and nobody wants pain and trouble, but a far wiser Brain than ours made it part of his scheme of things for a purpose. It is to make men of us.

Another thing to do when life gets hard is to square ourselves for a good fight. When some people encounter difficulty, they take the attitude of meek surrender. Instead of getting to their feet like men, they lie bewailing their fate. Some become cynical. They grow hard and bitter. This really is only another form of surrender. The effective way to react when life gets hard is not to surrender weakly and grow cynical, but to come up with a smiling face, ready for a new battle. The whole world cannot defeat a fighter. Edmund Vance Cook had the right idea. He writes:

> "You are beaten to earth?
>   Well, well, what's that?
> Come up with a smiling face.
>   It's nothing against you to fall down flat,
> But to lie there—that's disgrace.
>   The harder you're thrown, why, the higher you bounce;
> Be proud of your blackened eye!
>   It isn't the fact that you're licked that counts;
> It's how did you fight and why?"

It is not enough, however, to be a good fighter. Some people have learned to utilize a power greater than their own which is available to all of us.

That power is spiritual religion. It is the result of a

process by which the divine power flows into a man's life through an unimpeded channel from which obstructing will, selfishness, and sin have been removed. It is strange that we are so slow to accept the amazing power religion can give us for our daily lives when all the time in scientific invention men are opening up great new applications of power in the universe. Recently in a great research laboratory I saw a bar made from a new metallic compound called permalloy. It possesses such magnetic power that using it in communication systems over long distances on land and in cables under the sea, the number of transformers to amplify sound needed on present lines will be greatly reduced. My friend, who was showing me through the laboratory, performed an experiment with the permalloy bar in which he placed many and rather large pieces of metal on a table. He approached these pieces with one end of the bar, but there was no attraction. He moved the bar into many positions with no effect. Then he put the bar in the magnetic pole of the earth and so great was the attraction that the pieces of metal sprang to the end. When the bar was moved from the angle of the magnetic pole, listlessly they dropped off.

Life has no power when it is out of the magnetic pole of God. But when a man brings his life, by surrender of self, into contact with God so that divine power flows through him, life's elusive values spring to him with an ease that will amaze him. Do not mistake me —this is not to say religion is a get-rich scheme or that it will necessarily add material things. If you seek spiritual power for selfish purposes, it is of no purpose, for selfishness breaks the circuit. "Seek ye first the kingdom of God" (for its own sake) "and all these things" (that you need in God's sight) "will be added unto you."

But what do we mean by "success"? Of course our

definition, as I have just said, is not to be considered in terms of material values. Perhaps in fairness it should be mentioned that there frequently has been an unfair detraction of men who by ability and hard work have made themselves materially successful. It usually requires brains, energy, unremitting toil, and strength of character to accomplish that feat, and this is admirable in any man. Saying this, it of course does not follow that we mitigate or defend the abuses inherent in our system. An improved social order is the desire of every thoughtful man. Those abuses, however, can best be corrected by eliminating contumely toward personalities, and directing creative thought to the improper operations within our system.

A distinguished artist has a summer cottage down in Maine. He is especially fond of the glorious sunsets, and it is his custom to invite his friends to his veranda at the close of day to witness this spectacular display of nature. One evening he was describing, with his rare artistic gifts of appreciation, a sunset which had diffused the sky with exquisite coloring. A maid who had quietly been serving the company came to him and politely asked if she might run down the road to her home and tell her mother to look at the sunset. The artist said, "Why, certainly, but why do you want to ask your mother to look at the sunset? She has seen it many times." "Oh, no sir!" she replied. "I have lived here all my life, but I never saw a sunset until you came, and I want my mother to see it too."

This story raises a most curious problem. Why does life attain such varying quality in the hands of different people? Why is one person able to see a deeper and finer shading, a profounder meaning in life than another? Why is it that some people do so much more with life than others? We are all in the same world.

We see the same sky. We walk under the same stars; the same sunlight and rain fall upon our faces. Some people see in it deep and radiant beauty. Aware of its profound possibilities they make of life a result of superior quality. Others, seeing little in it and being blind to its larger possibilities, sadly enough are not so successful.

Now, I do not mean by this to analyze why one person attains a higher position or distinction in life than another. The problem does carry itself out there, however, for it is true that some people do accomplish more with the raw materials of life than others. The answer to that problem, however, is work and concentration plus a divine spark that was fanned. There is a divine spark in each of us, but many of us never fan it to a flame.

What we have been saying makes us ready now to answer the question, What do we mean by "success"? To me a very satisfactory definition of "success" is—to develop the soul in greatness—that surely is success. To see deeply into life, to taste deeply of it, to gain power over it, to stand in the midst of it—strong, perfectly integrated, kindly, spiritually minded—that is success. To make your life count for others, to contribute to human well-being—that is success. To compose your soul in peace and power—that is success. Some people achieve it; others fail. As I cast over in my mind the people of my experience who have made the most of their lives, I am reminded that they have been of all classes.

I remember a good woman, the mother of a large family, who lived in a little mill town in New England. She was always just a step or two ahead of poverty, and it required all of her housewifely ingenuity to stretch the few dollars over the needs of the family. She toiled from morning until night and then on into the night through long years. She sleeps now among the rocky hillsides of Rhode Island, but I shall never forget the glory of her face. It was seamed and wrinkled, but upon it was that ineffable radiance which came from an inner light deep within her soul. Rembrandt could have given such a face ageless immortality. She used to sit in her pew in the little church with her toil-worn hands folded on her simple dress. As she joined in singing the hymns of faith and listened to the sonorous and ancient words of the Scriptures, occasionally glancing in her direction, I knew that I was looking upon one who in the midst of life's rigorous vicissitudes had tapped the deep and inner secret of living. She went to the grave with nothing in her hands, but she left a fair name untarnished, good children who call her blessed, and the memory of a lovely personality. That is taking the raw materials of life and making a success of them.

I think of another person, a man worth many millions. If I were to mention his name, there are few to whom it would be unfamiliar. He made his money by selling a good product for an honest price. He was fair to the men who worked for him and they loved him. He knew scores of them by name and often visited them in their homes. My picture of him is a man, tall and erect, white hair, white beard, sitting in the church like some modern John Ruskin, drinking and tasting the waters of life. He used to arise in the prayer meeting and with a light on his face say, "Practice the presence of God." A young man, a lawyer in his city, told me once that he went to church very largely so he could look at the face of this great manufacturer. He said it gave him courage and strength to live an honest, clean-cut life. When this man died, his picture was carried in a three-column width on the front page of the paper. Underneath the picture was his name, together with the date of his birth and death and a single eulogistic line. The line did not say how much money he had or speak of the great industrial plant he had built or the social position he held. The line was a simple quotation from the Bible. It read, "Whatsoever things are pure." The poor woman and the millionaire had taken life as it came to them and with the raw materials each in his own way assembled a successful result.

In both of these people I noticed the predominance of one quality. Mr. James Truslow Adams put his finger on it in his inimitable description of John Adams. It is to the effect that these people had a profound faith in God as a living reality. In this they tapped hidden streams of beauty, strength and power. Religion for these people was intrinsically not a belief, not a doctrine, not a practice of certain acts, but conscious association with the divine spirit and life.

In a deep sense the secret of true success in living is the establishment of a real and vital personal contact with that ineffable being we call God. It need hardly be said that by this we mean something greatly to be differentiated from so-called nominal religion—not that the man with nominal religion is not a respectable member of society and often is a person of culture and refinement. He is usually a moral and upright man and would with some surprise say, "Why, what more do you want me to be?" His tragedy is not in what he has but in what he is missing. He may observe certain accepted religious forms and even much of its ethics, but there is a deeper factor—it is spiritual power in which we are interested. He says, "Look at the sins I have avoided, the mistakes I have not made." It is a religion of negative attainments. Suppose a man should blindfold himself and go on a walking tour of the Alps. He might come to the end of his blindfolded tour with the triumphant exclamation, "Look at the pitfalls I missed, the crevasse after crevasse which I avoided." Yes, of course, that would be quite a feat, but consider, also, the splendor which he failed to see —snow-capped peaks in the mystery of lingering sunset or bathed in the silvery light of the moon, the mists lifting like gossamer veils from noble summits, the far-flung vistas of great, dizzy valleys, the glint of sifted sunshine on laughing mountain streams—all this he would not see, its glory and exaltation he would not feel. His pride would be in what he had missed. Religion is like that for many people. The virtue in that kind of religious life is not to be too severely minimized, but if that is the most religion a man has, it is pretty thin fare on which to nourish his soul. Such a man surely stands in need of life's supreme experience, the art of making God real in his daily life.

The secret of this experience is to be found in a statement of Saint Paul's—He is "not far from every one of us: for in him we live, and move, and have our being." In those words the great apostle is telling us that God is not far removed, a vague and incomprehensible Being in some impenetrable heaven, but that he is so near to us, so completely shares the routine of our common life, our personalities are so blended with his own, that in effect we live in him and he in us. The fine quality of this relationship with God is illustrated in the life of a friend, an old man, who has searched long in spiritual things with deep success, who often says as naturally as though he were talking about a friend, "I said to God this morning." Another friend, an active and successful business man here in New

York, frequently—and particularly when important decisions are to be made, though he is surrounded by his associates—closes his eyes for a minute at his desk and asks God to be with him in that decision and help him. He tells me that God is with him all the day long in his office. The rich quality of the man's soul, the assurance of his faith, the obvious power of his life were explained fully when he told me this story. People of this stamp have hit upon the tremendous secret, that God can be real in daily life, and when he is, sources of power hitherto undreamed of are opened which add immeasurably to the effectiveness and happiness of a man's life.

What is the method by which we gain a sense of the reality of God in our everyday life? We are to realize that we are in God in a continuous creative process. "In him we live and move, and have our being." We make the mistake of believing that God created us in the beginning and has since abandoned us, cut us off from himself as separate entities, except when we beseech him across some great abyss. On the contrary, God's creative power ever goes on, recreating us when our strength abates and our spirits run low. Perhaps you have on the dashboard of your car an electric clock. At regular intervals you may hear it click. It is rewinding itself. In the old-fashioned dashboard clocks, it was necessary that they be wound by hand, but the electric clock is attached to an illimitable source of continuous power, and when its operation is at its low point, automatically the power renews itself from its boundless supply. The clock might say, to paraphrase Saint Paul's words, "Electricity is never very far from me, for in electricity I live, and move, and have my being."

In similar fashion the life lived in communion with

God experiences the constant renewal of the creating process by which strength of body, mind, and soul is never allowed to run down, but, on the contrary, is steadily and automatically restored as rapidly as it is drained off. All the time God is with you, filling you with his sustaining power. Think what that will do for you. Your sins—he will cover them all in a minute with his forgiving love. Your temptations—he will endow you with power over them. Your sickness—you can reach out and touch the hem of his garment. He will lay his healing hand upon you and your faith will prove to be an invaluable aid to medical science in giving you health. Your burdens—they will seem so light and easy to carry when along life's daily path you get his shoulder under your load. Your whole being will be conscious of the infusion of strange new power. Remember, Christ did not say he would give us a little and stingy life. He said, "I am come that ye might have life, and that ye might have it more abundantly." Why not take him at his word? He means it.

It is remarkable what God does for people who have a simple and childlike faith in him. One man who surrendered his life absolutely into God's hands wrote me saying, "I was amazed with what I found as I went deeper into spiritual realities." With this sort of religious life you can win the finest and most significant kind of success in living.

CHAPTER VII

OVERCOMING THE TENSION OF MODERN LIFE

THREE elderly and delightful ladies, sisters, from down South, who had not been far away from the peace and quiet of the old farm in forty years, made their first trip to New York. In the course of their visit they came to the Marble Church, which is set amidst the bustle and confusion at the heart of the city's busy life. Among the many questions they asked the sexton, who showed them about, was the puzzled query as to why the people in New York are always frantically rushing to catch a train when there will be another in two minutes. The oldest of the three, a very nice little old lady, said, "Why, land's sakes, down home we reckon if you don't get there today, you all surely will tomorrow." Vash Young, the well-known writer, picturesquely says that when "Mr. Jitters" excitedly tells him he will be late if he doesn't hurry, he turns to "Mr. Jitters" and calmly says, "So what!"

For the serenity and deliberateness which this homely philosophy represents most of us have a decided nostalgia. The nervous movement of life is generally characteristic of America in this hectic age, though it may still be retarded in some fortunate sections where the blight of high-geared metropolitan sophistication has not yet established a hold. An incident which might well serve as the great American anecdote on the basis of the truth it tells, was related to me recently. A woman, member of many clubs, sitter in at many a bridge table, veteran of not a few committee assign-

136

ments, living the usual American life of feverish activity, ended up finally, as many do, in a doctor's office. "Doctor, I'm all run down," she complained. To which he replied after an examination, "No, madam, the trouble is not that you are all run down but that you are all wound up." Contemplate the large number of people in middle life and indeed in their forties and even thirties, who succumb to heart trouble and other maladies related to tension and nervous ailments. As a people—"we are all wound up." The old deep peace of life is not in us. The whole jittery world, with its confusion and sinister uncertainties, has invaded the inner life of men more than we may think.

It is possible that this nation, having so large a proportion of urban dwellers, is losing that unhurried tempo which intimate association with nature fosters in men. The company of hills and valleys and great rivers and trees and babbling brooks and starlit nights is good for one's nervous system. "Consider the lilies of the field, how they grow; they toil not, neither do they spin." They do not get excited nor jittery; they simply go on growing with calm deliberateness, and when they are finished, it may be said of them "that even Solomon in all his glory was not arrayed like one of these." There is activity in nature twenty-four hours of the day, the most stupendous activity in the world; yet it is all accomplished in silence, without the creak of a pulley or the grating of a gear. We, on the other hand, put a lot of nervous excitement into deciding where we will spend the evening.

It is good for a man's soul, and his body and mind also, to associate with the silences of the natural world. There is nothing like a great peace-drenched mountain with its deep, sun-bathed, pensive valleys to calm him and slow him down. Let him linger in the hills long

enough and he will feel presently the cool touch of
Mother Nature's fingers drawing the fever from his life.
Like a restless, fretful child, she takes him to her bosom,
where presently the deep untroubled peace of her
heart transmits itself to his own. Then he rests in
perfect relaxation. The tension goes out of him. His
mind clears; the ability to think creatively returns;
decisiveness and strength are rejuvenated. The short
circuit of one's powers, brought about by the unceasing
tumult of mechanized, industrialized, socialized bee-
hives called cities, is corrected. The old firm connec-
tions with the deep springs of life are made fast once
again. He learns the subtle and reassuring truth that
life has a magnificent way of taking care of itself when
one is confidently calm about it. Calvin Coolidge may
have learned this truth from the rocky eternity of his
native Green Mountains. One day Mr. Coolidge lay
down for a nap in the executive office of the White
House. It was a busy day and important visitors and
matters of state waited while the President slept peacefully on past the time when he should have gone back
to work. His secretary tiptoed anxiously in and out,
hesitating to awaken his chief, yet noticeably concerned. At length Mr. Coolidge awakened, and, opening one eye, inquired with a sheepish look, "Is the country still here?"

Do not take things too seriously. The French have
a way of translating a certain well-known statement
from the Bible which is worthy of reflection. "Blessed
are the meek" is made to read—"Blessed are the debonair." That is a fine attitude to take—be debonair
about life. Do your best; work hard to justify good
fortune; and then trust yourself, trust life, and trust
the good God to take care of you.

Suppose the world is upset, that does not mean that

you should lose your poise. After all, the world you live in will be about as upset as you are. Your world on the outside is likely to reflect accurately your world on the inside. What if the world does appear upside down and you wonder what is going to happen to everybody and everything—remember that the world is like a rubber boat; it always manages somehow to right itself. The world is not going to pieces in your lifetime or in that of your children. Probably your grandfather thought it was too, but it didn't.

The best way to live is just to live. Don't look at life too closely. This is the era of self-examination and analysis. Books are rolling off the presses and being avidly read which do little more than make a psychological chart of you and me. We do need to know more about the human mind and why we do what we do, but most of us are becoming too inwardly self-conscious. People are destroying the flower garden of life by making botanical analyses of flowers when they should simply enjoy their beauty and fragrance. Forget your impulses and your desires and your complexes and your unexpressed self, and be a wholesome, natural human being and live like one.

There are times also to give thought, as a good citizen, to the affairs of the country, but that does not mean all the time. Don't take these perplexing problems to bed with you or to dinner with you. Go out and take a long look at the sky and the sea and the mountains and get peace into your mind. This will make us all happier and, as a matter of fact, will give us greater mental and spiritual efficiency with which to solve our problems.

I spent several summers on a lovely cedar-crested bluff overlooking a beautiful ocean bay. One evening I sat on the veranda, nursing my personal troubles.

I picked up a daily paper and what I read further deepened my gloom. "This country has seen its best days," I said, "and what in the world are we coming to?" Then I walked out under the trees and beheld a full moon bathing the earth in shimmering radiance. Across the bay fell a wide pathway of silver, sparkling on the rippling waters. The soft white clouds, which rumpled the sky, caught on their ends the moongleam slanting down the heavens, and were for all the world like great down pillows upon which God invited his children to rest. Far in the distance a sand dune lay white against the night. I studied the vast star-studded canopy above me, felt again the awe of its uttermost reaches, was caught by the spell of its eternity, and was struck with the idea that the same stars looked down upon Rome generations ago and upon many men before me in every age whose troubles, like mine, were very small in the presence of this majesty. Then I felt deep upon my heart "the peace that passeth understanding" and could almost hear a voice,

"Fear not, I am with thee; O be not dismayed,
For I am thy God and will still give thee aid."

I went to bed with the feeling that, after all, God could handle things.

Robert Louis Stevenson, who shook off the fell clutch of circumstance to become an expert in the art of living, gave us a sage bit of advice. "Sit loosely," he said, "in the saddle of life." I recall that Stevenson always had a childlike heart of faith. Perhaps it was that attitude which enabled him to sit loosely in the saddle of life, devoid of that tenseness and strain which breaks so many men.

I read a curious news item describing a tree which had been bent over by a hurricane a few years ago and was recently restored to its original position by another hurricane. It is a parable of that process in a man's life when, being hard hit by the storms of this day, he may recover himself by a strong inner force moving against adversity. That force is not so much one of violent activity as a confident trust that life, through good fortune and bad, is working out life's good. Take life calmly. Trust God entirely and the sum total of it will be that the good will outbalance the bad. Moreover, what we think is bad may often be the good in disguise. God, with his superior wisdom, knows more about working out our lives than we do and will accomplish it more effectively if we interfere less with him and give him a freer hand.

Chinese philosophers are of the opinion that every adversity is balanced by a corresponding advantage and that there is no bad luck or good luck. Lin Yutang, in *The Importance of Living,* puts this philosophy in the quaint story of an old man in China who had one horse and one son. The horse wandered away and was lost. The neighbors came in to sympathize with the old man on his bad luck. "How do you know it is bad luck?" he asked. Soon thereafter the lost horse returned with some wild horses and the neighbors gathered to congratulate him on his good luck. "How do you know it is good luck?" he asked. Having so many horses, the son took to riding, was thrown and broke his leg. The neighbors came to commiserate him on his bad luck. Again he queried, "How do you know it is bad luck?" Very shortly a war broke out and the son, because of his injury, did not have to go to war. Do your best, work hard, keep calm and trust God— that is the way to win in life.

Religion can help us overcome tension, for religion is designed to help us live day by day. Christianity should be as necessary to a man as the hat he puts on when he goes out for the day. If he can go off without it, obviously it does not mean much to him. One's religion should be a homely, well-worn article of everyday use. In our homes we have various types of articles. Some are purely ornamental, like some chairs that are seldom, if ever, used, but are for looks. Other articles are carefully put away, like the silver you received on your wedding day, and brought out only when company comes, or a special occasion arrives. Others are used every day. Without them we could not get along. They show signs of wear but they wear well, and as the years pass, we come to love them and depend upon them. Religion is like that. Some use it occasionally, but it is largely ornamental. It is not part of the main usage of their lives. They get it out for special occasions, as when they are hard-driven, or when trouble or death comes. For others it is like an old chair or an old glove or an old hat, without which one could scarcely get on. Religion is not something to be spoken about in an embarrassed and unnatural tone, but should be considered and treated as an everyday, natural, and necessary feature of man's life.

The practical value of religion in dealing with tension or fear or sickness or any of man's common problems has not been sufficiently emphasized. We have missed its power by thinking of it too much as a matter of ideaism or even idealism, when it should deal specifically with the realisms of life. Any person has the right to expect that he can go to church and find a power that will actually help him live day by day. If religion cannot go out of church with a man and walk down the street with him, of what practical good is it? A man's religion, to be worth its salt, must be able to do a day's work, and strap-hang at night in a crowded subway or bus without fainting. Everyday folk, everywhere, desperately need a revival of practical, everyday religion, to get into their hands some real spiritual tools they can use effectively. There are thousands of people in this country for whom life is needlessly difficult, and it is largely because they have forgotten, or never knew, how to make use of the religious power which the good God put here for their disposal.

We all need to learn the workable secret of strength by which to meet life successfully. How to be strong in trouble, in sorrow; how to be strong in personality, in moral problems, how to win in life's varying circumstances—that is what we want to know. Christianity has the answer. It possesses a definite technique and points the way to personal power for any man who will adopt it. The Bible lays down the formula in these words: "In quietness and confidence shall be your strength." Translating that into modern speech it means: Do not allow yourself to be fussed up by a situation. Do not get excited or panicky. Take it easily and calmly. No matter what the provocation, quietness is the proper atmosphere in which to meet any issue.

On her return from a trip to the Orient, my mother told of sitting on a balcony overlooking the starlit harbor at Singapore with James Hoover, pioneer missionary to Borneo, and Mrs. Hoover. They told her a thrilling story which admirably illustrates the quality of inner quietness, out of which they found the strength to meet the privations and dangers they had to encounter in those early days. Hoover, many years ago, took his young bride, a small portable organ, and a courageous heart, and sailed for Borneo. It was then still in large part the home of a savage people. When he died thirty years later, Borneo was a great commonwealth and the flag flew at half staff for a missionary. The first night he and his wife were on the island was spent in a little hut. Suddenly they were startled to see that they were surrounded by a great crowd of fierce-looking natives. There they were, alone in the jungle, a young white man and his wife, and all about them a horde of savages. They pressed closer, peering in the door. They talked among themselves in an unintelligible tongue. The situation was dangerous for the two young Americans. But they were equal to it, for they had learned the secret of inner quietness. They were strong enough for this crisis. Seating herself at her little organ, Mrs. Hoover began to sing and play the old hymns of the church. How strange and sweet they sounded in that far-off wilderness, these songs she had learned in the church back home across the seas! As she played, a curious thing happened. These warriors went to sleep, one by one, on their feet, which was their strange custom, she later learned. As slumber overcame them, they dropped like logs to the ground. This continued until all lay sleeping, strewn on the ground around the hut. With a deep thankfulness for their deliverance, the heroic young couple gave thanks to God, who is the source of quiet strength like this. And they needed that strength, for this remarkable experience was repeated for ten nights straight, but, as a result, a friendly contact was established with these rude people. The secret of nerve strength is to get your mind off the outer confusion and focus it on an inner citadel of quietness deep within your heart. If you keep the din and litter of the world out of that stronghold, then let the storms and dangers come—you are the match for them all. Regardless of how unstrung or nervous you may be, put Jesus Christ at the center of your life and you can

have a calmness and peace in your soul that will be the
most wonderful thing in the world. These words from
the Bible illustrate the inner peace religion offers:

> And behold, there arose a great tempest in the sea, insomuch
> that the ship was covered with the waves: but he was asleep.
>
> And his disciples came to him, and awoke him, saying, Lord,
> save us; we perish.
>
> And he saith unto them, Why are ye fearful, O ye of little
> faith? Then he arose, and rebuked the winds and the sea; and
> there was a great calm.

Some will say, "Oh, that's just a preacher talking," and
you won't accept Christ's calmness. But, remember,
it isn't the preacher who will suffer, but you. You are
perhaps a Christian, a church member. You believe
intellectually that what I am saying is true, but you
do not practice it, and so go on being nervous. The
Master can cure nerves for you today as in the long ago.

Our generation has been subjected to a terrific bom-
bardment of noise and emotional excitement. Like
water, dripping on a stone, noise and confusion will
draw off nerve control and set us on edge. In the city
of New York this has been recognized, and efforts are
being made to curb street noises, especially the honking of automobile horns. Some time ago I was driving my car through a crowded street when a woman
driver began to do unexplainable things which pre-
vented me from making what I considered a proper
turn at a corner. Somewhat impatiently, I suppose, I
began honking my horn at her, quite justifiably I felt. A
big, burly policeman started in our direction and I said
to myself with satisfaction, "He will tell this lady a
thing or two." But instead, he came to me and yelled:
"Hey, you gotta stop blowing that horn. Cut it out.
The mayor says we gotta stop this noise or we'll all go
crazy." Well, in a humbled and much-chastened spirit

I said to the officer, "The mayor is right." "Those who keep the peace of their inner selves in the midst of the tumult of the modern city," says Alexis Carrel, "are immune from nervous and organic disorders."

Men break physically and emotionally under never-ceasing tension and nervous agitation. Dr. George Crile, famous surgeon, is reported to have said that seventy-five per cent of the sickness in America is due to worry, and worry is a form of tension. Enrico Caruso had a dinner table trick which he used to delight in executing for the pleasure of his fellow diners. Holding a fragile glass aloft, its narrow stem between his thumb and forefinger, he would sing the ascending scale until he would reach a certain high note. Sounding this high note repeatedly for a moment, it would cause the glass to shatter into bits. I am told that the most severe test given to an automobile at the proving ground is to drive the car at high speed over a smooth concrete pavement. The high-frequency vibrations thus set up attack hidden parts in the mechanism much more rapidly and with greater damage than a rough road which would to the layman seem to offer more possibility of harm.

If tension can so profoundly disturb a mechanism of metal construction, how damaging must be its effect upon the mind and nerve cells and heart of that mechanism of flesh and blood and personality called man. To win in life we must solve this problem of overcoming the tension of modern life.

Beyond the causes of tension which have already been referred to are others to which attention should be called. For the most part, these causes are in the mind and emotions. We ought not to blame the nervous mechanism of our bodies but, rather, blame the mind that controls that mechanism. The brain may be likened to the central office of a telephone system, the nerves to telephone lines running to each cell in the body. When nervousness develops, the trouble is not with the nerves, as we often incorrectly suppose. We say, "Our nerves are shot to pieces." But that is not so, for the nerves themselves are not damaged. It is the mind that is at fault, for the mind controls the nerves. Back of the nerve machinery is this unseen worker called the mind, which presides like an operator over the telephone system and uses this wonderful mechanism to control the body. Any so-called nervous condition, from the simplest case of fidgets to the most pronounced hysteria, is caused predominantly by some state of mind rather than by any trouble with the nervous system. If you are suffering from tension, the chances are the cause is not your body. The trouble is with your thoughts. Our emotions are caused by the thoughts we think. That is why religion is so effective in curing tension, because emotion causes tension and religion deals with emotion.

Fear is one of the greatest causes of nervousness. If you are nervous, if your nerves are on edge so that you are ready to "fly to pieces," if you are under tension, it may be that you are afraid of something. A simple illustration will show how fear and worry cause nervousness. I recall the first time I made a speech. There was a lump in my throat caused by the contraction of muscles and the drying up of the salivary glands. My knees shook and I was alternately hot and cold all over. I remember a little girl sitting in the front seat, who shouted out in a loud tone as I stood with my knees shaking, "Oh, look at his knees shaking!" What was the matter with those knees? Fear had laid a grip on my mind, and the messages sent by the mind over the nerves down to the knees were so indecisive

that the knees could do nothing but wobble. My
trouble was not in my nervous system but in my mind.

Sin and remorse will also cause tension. Psychologists tell us that unrepented sin—that is, sin that is not
removed, is responsible for many nervous breakdowns.
It is the devastating effect of a sense of guilt. A college
student once came to me who was actually physically
sick from nervousness. He had committed a sin. He
had done something which his social set had said was
quite the thing. They laughed at this thing as being
a sin, for they said that sin was out of date, so he threw
over his ideals and committed the sin. Afterward he
discovered he had a pain in his mind, and he couldn't
get away from it. It made him so nervous he couldn't
sleep; he could not eat; he could not do his work;
and, in fact, was rapidly going to pieces. He came to
me as a minister and confessed his sin and made possible the reopening of his life to the flow of spiritual
vitality. His nervousness ceased, tension subsided, and
subsequently he could work effectively and his whole
physical and mental life was restored. Practical experiences of this sort are evidence of the amazing power
of a wholesome spiritual life to heal the disease of
nervous tension.

The persistence of inner conflicts is a direct cause of
tension in men's lives. Some lines from the Indian poet,
Rabindranath Tagore, come to mind:

"Who is this that follows me in the silent dark?
 I move aside to avoid his presence but I escape him not;
 He makes the dust rise from the earth with his swagger;
 He adds his loud voice to every word that I utter;
 He is my own little self, my lord."

Many are indeed hounded by the inner self. They
are a battleground of conflicting impulses. The story
is a universal one. It has long been the theme of the

novelist and the preacher. Of late it has become the
concern of the physician. An acute conflict, long sustained, may break a man, destroying his powers of
effectiveness and causing his life to fall in about him.
Pathetic souls are they in whom there is a never-ceasing
tumult of inner conflict. They cry out for peace, but
there is no peace. Like the ghost of Hamlet's father,
thoughts which we have inhibited and desires which
we have restrained come marching out of the depths
of the unconscious to capture the citadel of our lives.
Fires burn beneath the surface of our lives which are
constantly getting us into trouble.

Over fifty years ago some miners in a Middle-Western
state, to satisfy a grievance, real or imagined, ignited a
carload of coal and pushed it down the long shaft of
the mine. All ablaze, it struck the bottom and as it
burned transmitted itself to the layers of coal within
the earth. For fifty-two years now that fire has burned,
consuming twelve million tons of coal, and has burned
over an area of ten square miles. Now and then a road
will fall in, its undergirding having been eaten out
by fire. Men and animals have been asphyxiated by
the noxious gases which have escaped through fissures
in the earth. Some curious, and even humorous, results have followed. A farmer dug up roasted potatoes
from one of his fields, but the principal result has been
to reduce property values and cause suffering and sorrow. All efforts to quench the fire have been fruitless.

That is a parable of human life. People in a moment of anger or of thoughtlessness, or in a moment
of yielding to some temptation, start fires deep in their
souls which they cannot put out. Gradually these
fires eat away the power and strength of their lives.
Wistfully I see them coming in and out of the church,
in and out of our conference room, looking for peace

and the deep joy of release from their inner conflicts. They are seeking some cooling water that will put out the fires that burn in their souls. Because he knew all this so well, because he is the Supreme Physician of all confused and distressed humanity, Jesus Christ once said, "Come unto me and I will give you rest."

I have often wondered why Jesus Christ enjoys such a profound hold upon all sorts and conditions of people. I believe one reason is that he is a perfectly balanced Personality. In him are no obsessions or quirks. In him are no conflicts. He is a perfectly integrated Personality. He is strong and peaceful and offers those qualities to us. The quality of rest that Christ gives us is not a sheltered indolence, but the infectious strengthening of spiritual health. From the man who puts his faith in him he removes every barrier to inner power. No longer is it necessary to dissipate energies in never-ending inner conflicts. Those conflicts having been solved, a man is now able to make a unified impact against life.

In my capacity as a clergyman, a calling the function of which is the cure of souls, I have seen time and again people like these get complete release by surrender to Jesus Christ. Freed, through faith in Christ, from the crippling, dwarfing imprisonment of their conflicts, they have become successful in their work, happy in their living and joyful in all their relationships. The surest way to escape inner conflict of any sort is to become a real Christian. Genuine faith in, and practice of, the Christian life will give you relief from yourself.

The Christian religion helps us to overcome our inner conflicts by giving us workable faith. It may be difficult for you to have this kind of faith. What is the answer? Simply accept faith. Believe you have it

and you will have it. That, you see, is itself faith. A
wise man once advised John Wesley, saying, "Preach
faith until you get faith, and then you will preach faith
because you have faith." When one has a genuine
faith, he will act as though he had Christ's power, and
the result of that assumption will be that he will have
Christ's power. The reason many people do not get
more value from religion is that they do not have
enough faith in it, or are too timorous to practice it.
The effective procedure is to say, "I want spiritual
power; I want the ability to overcome myself and my
conflicts." Then ask God for it, believing that through
your faith, and according to your need, he will give it
to you. Having asked him for it, believe that you
have it, act as though you have it, and the deep tendency will be for you to possess it. The Bible tells us in
Saint Mark 11. 24—"What things soever ye desire, when
ye pray, believe that ye receive them, and ye shall have
them."

A British psychologist says that when we wish to
control an emotion, we should simulate its opposite.
That is, when you are depressed and wish to be happy,
throw back your shoulders, take a deep breath, and
laugh as heartily as you can. That procedure, foolish
as it may appear to be, by the simulation of happiness
does tend to dissipate depression. If you are afraid,
simulate courage, act as though you had courage, and
you will have courage. Therefore if, torn by inner
conflicts and harassed by a disorganized personality,
an individual wants the power which religion alone
can give him, let him by an act of faith simulate spiritual power and it will tend actually to come to him.
This is a subtle and genuine principle of the religious
life practiced by all too few people, but those who do
practice it enthusiastically testify to its validity.

The petty irritations of everyday life add their contribution to the tension under which we live. The major difficulties and adversities of this life are met by most men with courage and fortitude. Sorrow, hardship, and disappointment by their very magnitude call forth reserve powers from some deep center of personality which prove adequate for the crisis. But often the very people who successfully master the greater problems and troubles of life go down to defeat before the petty irritations of everyday existence.

Irritations are roughly of two kinds: First, there are inner annoyances. They show themselves as the result of a pressure or tension in the mind and subsequently in the nervous system. An outward manifestation is often in the form of a rasping irascibility. The individual is easily upset by little things and flies into outbursts of temper out of all proportion to the size of the stimulus. An example is a man kicking a chair against which he has stumbled or breaking a golf club on the ground after a poor shot. Often it takes the form of a vague sense of dissatisfaction, a subconscious feeling that something is wrong or unpleasant.

Second, there are outer irritations, such as the annoyance of unpleasant circumstances, as, for example, like work that one does not enjoy or that becomes monotonous. A committee from the British House of Lords, making an investigation of industrial plants, noticed in one factory that whereas all other workmen were pushing their wheelbarrows before them, one man was disconsolately pulling his behind him. One of the Lords asked him why he thus deviated from the usual practice. The workman's reply was eloquent in its cogency. Tipping his grimy cap, he replied, "Because, my lord, I'm tired of seeing the blasted thing."

Another form of outer irritation is the friction that

sometimes develops between people due to malad-justed or clashing dispositions. Whether irritations proceed from inner tension or outer circumstances, the fact remains that they do exist, and our problem is to learn a workable technique for mastering them. Theory, however brilliantly projected, will not satisfy the demand represented in this problem. We want a practical, usable answer to a question faced every single day from morning until night. Develop at the center of your life an inner quietness or central calm like the quiet and order which prevails on the bridge of a vessel in a storm at sea. The ocean is in tumult, the wind roars a gale. On deck everything that is not lashed fast is uncontrollable. The passengers are dis-tressed and anxious. But on the bridge and in the steersman's cabin there is an entire absence of con-fusion. Every man goes quietly about his duty with scarcely a word spoken. Nobody loses his head. Like a thing alive, the great ship makes her way through the tempest to a safe harbor. In her quietness is her strength.

A person can make his way through all manner of confusion if deep in the center of his personality is this area of peace and inner quietness. This citadel of inner calm will serve one well, for to it he may retire and find rest when hard-pressed. There he may gain renewed strength so that he will not be worn out by the dissipation of his energies in little irritations. Em-phasis on an inner calmness in nowise indicates that one should retire from the give-and-take of the world nor that he shall not possess personal force. On the contrary, this inward peace is the true source of a man's strength. A cyclone tearing with immeasured power across the sky derives its energy from a calm area at its center. In that place of absolute stillness power

is generated for cyclonic activity. Many people who
have learned the deep secret of religion have developed
this inner calmness by a type of faith which believes
that all things work together for good and who refuse,
therefore, to become panicky or nervously agitated and
have thus been able to overcome the pressure which
eventuates in irritation.

Saint Paul describes this process in felicitous phrase
—"the peace of God that passeth all understanding."
Out of this attitude toward life one evolves the art of
detachment. He develops the elevated mind which
enjoys the capacity to rise majestically above little
things. Such a person can make his way with unfail-
ing urbanity and generosity of spirit among the fretting
circumstances which surround him. These petty irritations and annoyances may sting him a bit, but they
never penetrate his defenses, nor rob him of his poise,
nor interfere with his imperturbable self-control.
There is an old Latin proverb which I have always
liked. It illustrates admirably the type of mind I am
describing. It says, "The eagle does not catch flies."

The quality of calm inner detachment should work
itself out in a sense of perspective or proportion. It
teaches one not to take things, including himself, too
seriously. Allow your explosion to take the form of a
laugh and the power of the irritation is broken. A
hearty laugh is an excellent tension breaker, and it is
available instantly to the wise man who practices its
use. This does not mean one should become one of
those bores who goes about with a Cheshire cat grin
upon his face, but it does evaluate highly that person
who has learned to deflate life's pompous strut.

I have noted of late a strong tendency for those into
whose lives the strain and tension of modern living has
entered to turn wistfully and hopefully back to the

healing waters of religion, to the balm of Gilead, to Christ who alone has the skill to restore peace to their disoriented and troubled lives. They open up the pages of a Book, long unused by many of them, and read: "Come unto me all ye that labor and are heavy laden, and I will give you rest." They sit down and meditate upon great statements like this: "In quietness and confidence shall be your strength," and they find the restoration of their lives, for truly as the old psalm says, "He restoreth my soul." And that is just why modern people need Christ; he restores their souls. "Peace I give unto you," Christ offers. Get that into your life and what a transformation will take place! The old haunting fears that have troubled you so long, the sense of panic with which you have awakened on so many dreary mornings, the dark and heavy burdens which have crushed your spirit, the unremitting tension, will fall away like the old dead leaves from a tree in the spring when new life surges within it.

A man in his early forties, following a life in which religion, either formal or of the deeper spiritual quality, had no place, broke finally under the strain of days of business and nights of artificial emotional stimulation. His nerves jangly and jumpy, with a vague but pronounced emptiness in his heart, he turned to the church as a sort of last resort. There he found that Christianity deals directly with human needs and provides a faith and practical technique by which lives at loose ends may find inner harmony and power. "I want peace and a way out of the strain which, unless I find relief, will surely break me," he declared. I asked him if he had consulted a physician. He replied that he had, and the doctor told him he was organically sound, but that if the tension in his mind was not corrected, it would soon manifest itself in serious physical trouble.

As I talked with him, I thought of how Christ used to
speak peace to men like him and heal them. I wondered if he could not still do it. I determined to find out,
to apply sincere faith. I asked him to join with me in
prayer, and I prayed something like this: "Lord, long
ago in a storm on Galilee thou didst still the waves,
and there was a great calm. You also gave peace to
troubled lives. We believe your hand retains its
ancient skill. Here is a modern twentieth-century man
whose life is filled with storm and stress. He is facing
a nervous breakdown. He puts his life in thy kindly
hands. Speak peace to his soul. Heal him if it be thy
will." If this man could today speak to you, he would
say what he has often told me, that the prayer was
answered, not all at once but gradually over the weeks;
like a great hush, there came upon his life a healing
touch which gave him peace and with it the boundless
strength of a new life. Explain it as you will, Christ
healed this man of his affliction just as he healed men
like him in Galilee long ago. He said he often had
prayed but it did no good until that day. "What made
it happen then, do you think?" I asked him. "Because
that day somehow I meant it with all my soul and
seemed to believe Christ would help me." You see,
his faith reached high enough this time to close the
circuit and God's power instantly flowed through him.
His faith made him whole.

In healing our nervousness and in giving us a great
calm in our souls the practice of spiritual Christianity
does two things for us: First, it puts us in touch with
the power of God. We live and work on streams that
dry up because they come from within ourselves. We
need to attach the machinery of our lives to that great
river, which is forever full, which never runs dry, because it has far-off fountains that continually feed it.

It is the river of God's power. This stream flows full
of healing power and strength for any man who will
attach his life to it. Such a man is not the prey of fear
or worry or anxiety, because he knows he has resources
of strength by which he can meet life and triumph
over it. He becomes poised and calm and unruffled.
His powers are unhampered and ever at his disposal.
Men like this do things of worth-while accomplishment,
while lesser men fritter away their vital energies in
worry and nervous tension.

Do the best you can and trust your own inner power
and fear no evil. Drive the dark shadows out of your
mind, the foolish concerns of what may happen, the
empty fears, for they are empty, most of them; put
them all aside, have faith in God, have faith in life,
have faith in yourself, and all will be well. E. Stanley
Jones has a fine phrase called "the leisured heart"
which, as he points out, Christ gives to those who
fully surrender to him.

A second way in which Christ helps us to master our
nerves is by the gift of a mystic peace of a quality found
nowhere else in this world. There is something deep
in the touch of Christ that gives a peace which is well
described as passing understanding. Nature, as has
been pointed out, has the gift in large measure. There
is a place on Long Island along a foam-washed beach
where I am always aware of peace. The long rollers
dash their spray upon the sands, where no crowds ever
come. The high sand dunes are covered with beach
grass waving in the breeze. There is a sparkle and
glitter of clean waters coming from out a vast deep,
the tang of salt air, the low throb of the mighty ocean.
But that is not to compare with the peace of Christ.
"My peace I give unto you, not as the world giveth give
I unto you. Let not your heart be troubled." This

deep peace makes it possible to avoid agitation or tension because of anything that may happen today. It also adds a calm faith in tomorrow. William Allen White expressed it in a fine statement. "I am not afraid of tomorrow, for I have seen yesterday and I love today."

To win in life you must have an inward calm and confidence, a poised assurance, and the way to it is a simple faith in God. This will enable you to take life in your stride and the troubles and vicissitudes which you will meet will never triumph over you.

CHAPTER VIII

THE END OF TEARS

WHAT is a tear? The dictionary defines it as a small drop of the watery fluid secreted by the lachrymal gland of the eye, but that isn't really a tear at all. A tear is agony in solution. The tear is universal. This is so truly a fact that the world is often referred to as "This vale of tears." The Bible says, "In the world ye shall have tribulation," and it is so. Death, disappointment, sickness, hope deferred, hardship, all leave their trail of tears.

Here is a mother taken by death from home and the bosom of her family, and there are tears. Here is a baby snatched from a mother's arms and carried on angel's wings back to the God who gave it, and there are tears. Here are a husband and wife, companions and comrades along life's way, one of whom stumbles and falls in the journey and the other must go on alone, and there are tears. Death leaves its track of tears. As we look around us in these difficult days we see tears everywhere. Here is a man disappointed and frustrated by conditions over which he has no control. He tries to keep a sturdy heart, but even so, there are tears. Here is a family with savings nearly gone and all they have labored and struggled for, placed in jeopardy. They are not beaten, but there are tears. It has apparently ever been so, that all ages of men have known the experience of tears.

There is a fellowship of sorrow in which every generation partakes. As we suffer now, so have those before us, and our sorrows are softened by the sympathy of pilgrims who have preceded us. On the campus

159

of Cornell University, facing the lake, is a marble bench, presented by a graduating class years ago, on which is inscribed for the benefit of modern students, these words: "To those who shall sit here rejoicing, and to those who shall sit here lamenting—greeting and sympathy. So have we done in our time."

But our thought deals with the end of tears. It is described in a passage of surpassing beauty in the book of Revelation—"They shall hunger no more, neither thirst any more; neither shall the sun light on them, nor any heat. For the Lamb which is in the midst of the throne shall feed them, and shall lead them unto living fountains of waters: and God shall wipe away all tears from their eyes."

That is a great statement. I have always been fascinated by it, and have read it many times in places of sorrow. Its sonorous words breathe of the heights and depths of eternity, and yet there is in it the tenderness of a father leaning in comfort over a hurt child. What does it tell us of the end of tears? This passage refers directly to the afterlife, yet there is in it a meaning of present significance. God wipes away tears here and now, and he does it through people. His agents in eliminating tears are people who have a sense of social responsibility; who have a haunting sense of the sufferings of humanity. Goethe is said to have remarked that if he were God, the sins and woes of the world would break his heart. That is exactly what they did to God, and one of the great things is that a man like Goethe could feel the divine sense of sorrow. Sadly enough, there are all too few people who have developed that social sensitiveness by which their hearts are touched and their activities inspired by the still, sad music of humanity. William Howard Taft once put his finger squarely on the trouble. He said, "Too many people do not care what happens as long as it does not happen to them." The great benefactors of the human race, who, like Jesus Christ, have taken upon their shoulders the cross of mankind, have been those who have made all human suffering personal. It gives us a clearer understanding of the hardships some men bear, when, even imaginatively, we put ourselves in their places.

Ask yourself a question something like this: "Suppose I lived in a sordid, smelly tenement house, where the surroundings, in their stark unloveliness, kill, one by one, the fine flowers of hope and culture and development. Suppose, I say, that I lived like that." The answer is, "Well, some people do, aye, many people do." Ask yourself another personal question: "Suppose I lost my position and watched my savings, slight as they are, gradually diminish until I came down to my last dollar, and tramped the streets in vain, seeking work, and terror, with its cold and icy fingers, gripped my heart. Suppose, I say, that was my situation." Some people have that very problem to face. It makes a difference, doesn't it, when you take upon yourself, in a personal way, what other people suffer? The glory of this common humanity of ours is that there are some people who get near enough to the heartbeat of suffering mankind to feel that pain in themselves. Through them, God wipes away tears from their eyes.

Consider, for example, the career of Jane Addams. Years ago in London on a business trip with her father, in Whitechapel one night she saw something that made her the servant of the poor. In a crowded street, where meat was being sold for a pittance because it was spoiled, she saw the emaciated, bony hand of a poor woman reach up under a flaring light for a piece of meat. The sight of that hand broke her heart, and then and there she consecrated herself to the less fortunate. Years of a tender ministry bespoke the sincerity of that consecration. She helped God wipe away tears from their eyes.

Much may be done in this world to dry people's tears, but the deep, fundamental sorrows of mankind, death, separation from loved ones, and the mystic, poignant sadness of human life remain. Only God can wipe away tears which spring from those deeper fountains. Add to man every worldly benefit and comfort and still he will experience sorrow and heartache in this present world. At long last, says the Bible, God shall himself wipe away every tear from our eyes.

Never shall I forget one stormy winter day when we had gathered at the funeral service of an aged minister, who, having suffered much trouble in his life, now rested from his labors. His hands were peacefully folded, and the suggestion of a smile was on his face. His life had been a hard one, but we could see that all the anxiety, pain, and sorrow were now over. One of his contemporaries, an old minister with snow-white hair, stood up to pay him tribute. The storm beating about the church almost drowned out his feeble voice as he began to speak quietly. As he spoke, however, new vigor came to him, and as the wind blew without and snow piled against the windows we listened, in the hush of a great awe, as in a manner I have never heard before nor since, he slowly repeated the solemn lines of Tennyson's immortal poem—

> "Sunset and evening star,
>   And one clear call for me!
> And may there be no moaning of the bar,
>   When I put out to sea."

He finished, and then, looking down at his dead comrade, spoke his name and said, "At last, my dear friend, God has wiped away all tears from your eyes." As I listened, in my heart I knew that he spoke the truth. There is an end of tears for us all.

To win in life involves the ability to rise above the sorrow and pain of human existence. Man's amazing discoveries and inventions have failed to relieve him of sorrow. In some respects physical pain has been mitigated by advancing medical science, and increasing comforts have been placed at our disposal by scientific invention. At the same time, many of these inventions, such as airplanes and machinery of war, have probably brought a greater sum total of human misery to the world than ever existed in history. The social disorganization following upon the development of the mechanized era has through financial panic and widespread unemployment made a deep hurt in man's spirit. Nor has scientific alleviation of physical pain meant any reduction in the place of man's most acute suffering, that of pain in the spirit. Not yet has been invented a gadget to take the anguish out of a human heart. That requires a skill far beyond the capacity of the physical sciences. It demands a wizardry superior to that of Edison or Marconi or any of the modern wonder-workers. That genius is reserved for an alchemist of the spirit named Jesus Christ. An old Irish woman living in a crowded city said that when the weight on her heart became too heavy to bear, she "went and had a cup o' tea with Father Moike." To the kindly old priest, vicar of Christ, she poured out the burden and pain of her life and went away with a light heart and new courage. It was not the priest who worked the alchemy nor the psychological effect of confession, but, rather, the operation of simple faith in the great healer of the human spirit.

One of the profound sorrows of this world is the loss by death of our loved ones. It is a universal grief, for everywhere the funeral cortege winds solemnly to God's acre. No day passes but human minds wistfully ask the question, "Will we meet our loved ones again?" One tragic night, twenty-six years ago, a mighty ship was crossing the north Atlantic. It was her maiden voyage. She was the pride of Britain's fleet, the greatest ship afloat. Her name was *Titanic*. Gay parties were in progress. Laughter and music floated out over the starlit waters. Everyone was happy. The magic of the silver moonlight turned the water into phosphorescence. The great engines throbbed steadily on as, with lights ablaze, the noble vessel glided through calm seas. Gradually the air grew chill, but those on deck thought it only the freshness of a spring night. Suddenly a dark green thing of terrifying size loomed dead ahead in the path of the ship. Vainly bells rang. The steersman put the wheel hard over, but no power on earth could stop that momentum or avoid the crash. There was no escape. Then came scenes of immortal heroism. The innate nobility of human beings facing eternity was proved once again. The ship's lights went out, and on her slanting decks hundreds were hushed by the solemn strains of the band playing "Nearer, My God, to Thee." This story, one of the most tragic in the experience of our time, brings to mind the solemn philosophy of Charles Frohman, who, on the deck of the sinking Lusitania, said to a group of friends: "Why fear death? Death is only a beautiful adventure."

To be proficient in the art of living we must know somewhat about dying, for, strangely enough, dying is an important factor in living. Death, we believe, is but a stage in life, a change into a different form of existence—like the caterpillar changing into the butterfly or a door opening into a larger life. In a world of wonders like the radio, the airplane and television, to mention only a few modern miracles, the possibility of life after death grows apace. It is remarkable how dogmatic and unscientific some scholars can become at times. For example, the British scientist who, some years ago, said, "At death the spirit of man will be extinguished like a candle flame." Of course the question is, "How does he know that? Where is his evidence?" The plain fact is, he knows nothing about it for, as Shakespeare pointed out, he is dealing with "the undiscovered country from whose bourne no traveler returns." Scientists like this are now rather out of date, for the greater scientific men tend to reset theism and more spiritual thinking at the center of their explanation about the universe and though, manifestly, they have not proven it and perhaps cannot catagorically do so, their thinking is in the direction of faith in immortality.

It is natural that we should have an insatiable curiosity concerning the afterlife. When Henry Thoreau lay dying at Concord, his friend, Parker Pillsbury, sat by his side and said, "Henry, you are so near to the border now, can you see anything on the other side?" To which Thoreau, with a feeble smile, replied, "One world at a time, Parker." This may have been satisfying to the reflective mind of the sage of Walden Pond, but men do look with longing into that other land where their loved ones have gone. They have watched them go like ships, disappearing down the bay. They have stood and watched as they sailed into the great unknown and have asked, "Shall we meet our loved ones again?" The desire is a very normal one. In the long course of the years human lives grow close together. The sound of a voice becomes precious—the touch of a hand, the pressure of a step, the silent presence is a benediction. Here are a husband and wife, beloved companions of a long journey—will they meet again? Here also mother and father, sons and daughters, bound together in the tender relationship of a family. Mother and father grow old and fade back into the dust, leaving heartbreak and a sense of loneliness and longing in the hearts of children where they will be cherished as long as life shall last. Will they see those dear faces again in some happier country?

There is nothing in this world so inexorable as time. "Change and decay in all around we see." Nothing remains as it is. Recently I revisited a little town in Ohio where, as a boy, I spent many happy summers at the home of my grandparents. I walked the old familiar streets, noting that houses, great to my once childish eyes, were now small and unimpressive, and I contemplated solemnly the evidences of change everywhere. I missed many people who once were prominent citizens of the place, but who had joined that ever-moving and innumerable caravan which had gone over the hill into the sunset. Many whom I had known in the vigor of their lives were now broken and bowed with the weight of years. I came finally to the home of a beloved aunt, where I had played with my cousins and my brothers in days long gone. I visited the old-fashioned barn, to me happily unchanged, and the haymow, once a place of mystery. I passed through the kitchen and into a pantry where hungry boys never failed to find the most delicious cookies in the state of Ohio, always awaiting us in a jar conveniently placed. But the hands that made them and the voice that sang about her work were gone and the place was sad and strangely empty, for what is a house when the dear personalities which made it a home are gone?

But the high spot of my visit was when I rounded the corner of the house and found to my delight that the thing for which I was looking was still there. It was an old-fashioned swing, with opposite seats and made of metal. Well do I remember when, bright and shiny, it was set up for the first time more than twenty-five years ago. We boys played railroad train in it. I always wanted to be the conductor so that I could take up the money—only it was not money, but pins, I believe. But that was all long ago. Now the old swing will no longer swing. The platform has broken loose and rests on the ground. No longer is it bright and shiny, but rusty and frail. Touching it made it weave precariously. Time, I reflected, has done this—time, which makes everything old and frail. Time, which works this havoc with things, does it also to people, and one by one, I knew that those I love would go from me. Is this the end of all our happy associations? Everywhere the question intrudes upon our minds in poignant wistfulness—"Shall we meet our loved ones after death?" I believe that we shall; I am sure that we shall. There is no shadow of a doubt about it in my mind, but I cannot prove it for the skeptical mind. I cannot prove it any more than another can disprove it. You cannot prove a thing like this as you can a diagram in geometry or a case at law. There is no method by which it can be either proved or disproved. You simply know a truth like this by faith. Something whispers it to your heart in the form of a deep intuition or conviction. I could, of course, work out a satisfactory philosophical basis for my faith, and it would be a system of logic quite as sound as that which anyone could work out against it—more so, I am confident. The logic is convincing to me, but if I had to accept it solely upon cold logic, it would mean little. As Martineau said, "We do not believe in immortality because we can prove it, but we try to prove it because we cannot help believing it."

Thus it is not my purpose in this chapter to attempt to prove the thesis of immortality; only to state my faith. I believe in immortality with a strong and steady conviction. I believe that when my loved ones pass into the great beyond, I shall see them again. I believe there is an end of tears.

Only you can convince yourself of immortality, for it is not a demonstration nor a proposition. It is, and must forever be, a deep conviction or instinct. "The faith of immortality," says Horace Bushnell, "depends upon a sense of it begotten and not an argument for it concluded."

I can tell you, however, how to deepen your faith. There are two things you must do: the first is to look deeply into the soul of man, not man as he appears to be but man as he is in his heart; the second is to get near to the heart of God. When one examines the human heart at close range, he becomes aware of a greatness and a fundamental goodness. Superficial observation of man makes apparent his many imperfections, but a deeper study reveals a grandeur which Emmanuel Kant said filled him with constantly increasing admiration and awe so that he compared the inner worth of man to the glory of the starry heavens.

Surely, also, no writer ever knew men with such sure instinct as did Shakespeare. The Bard of Avon is the supreme literary genius of the world because of his uncanny knowledge of man. He says, "What a piece of work is man! how noble in reason! how infinite in faculty! in form and moving how express and admirable! in action how like an angel! in apprehension how like a god; the beauty of the world! the paragon of animals!"

Looking into man in this manner we shall surely find
ourselves in agreement with Oxenham—

"In every soul of all mankind
Somewhat of Christ I find,
    Somewhat of Christ—and thee;
    For in each one there surely dwells
That something which most surely spells
Life's immortality."

The second way to get the feel of immortality in
your soul is to get up close against the heart of God.
As the stern negatives, heavy doubts, fear of death,
fears of losing loved ones come like dismal fog into
your soul, get close to God's heart, look up into his
face, and you will know.   Long ago when I was a little
fellow, with my father and mother I was on the old
Ohio River boat, *The Island Queen,* coming at night
into her dock.   It was a stormy night and some confusion had arisen in warping the boat into her pier,
which sent a near panic through the people.   The tense
atmosphere, the storm clouds, the lightning—all com-
bined to put fear into the heart of a little boy.   I looked
over the side of the vessel, down to the dark, swirling
waters, and was afraid.   I can remember even now with
healing comfort snuggling close up against the side of
my father and looking into his face; whereupon he
smiled confidently at me and I was no longer afraid.
In similar manner, as our little craft makes its way
over the stormy sea of life and as we feel the mist in our
faces and know we are nearing the place, like Browning
in "Paracelsus" one may say—

"If I stoop
Into a dark tremendous sea of cloud,
It is but for a time; I press God's lamp
Close to my breast; its splendor, soon or late,
Will pierce the gloom; I shall emerge one day."

As the veteran pilot can hear the far-off sound of bells above the storm, which others cannot discern, so he who knows the ways of God and man can catch intimations of eternal coastlines.

Thus he who has looked deeply into the heart of man and God may not, it is true, understand all, but he has caught reflections, foretokens, intimations of immortality. It is unwise, for the reason that it is futile, to approach this matter scientifically. In the first place, it is out of the realm of science; it is a beyond science question. It is beyond science because science deals and can deal only with the facts of the physical world which can be measured, weighed, accurately observed and classified. The fact of immortality belongs not to the natural sciences but to philosophy and religion. Moreover, scientific considerations for or against the belief in immortality are practically meaningless. Psychical research, it is true, tries to point out verifiable testimony, but the evidence advanced is scanty at best and unreliable. Nor should we give much consideration to scientific disproofs concerning immortality, for usually they are not worth the paper they are written on. The simple fact is that science has no data.

When we approach this question from the purely scientific point of view, the best we can do is to balance one set of evidence against the other and then deduce what we will, which, of course, leads us instantly back into the region of faith. It might be remembered that science itself depends upon intimations, inspirations, even faith, for, as Lord Kelvin told us long ago, when the scientist comes to the end of demonstration, he must take what he calls a mortal leap to come finally to truth. Thus, if in scientific inquiry the gleam of intimations leads the scientist on, so may we in this field have confidence in the validity and accuracy of our intimations of immortality. So Lowell, in "The Cathedral," is dealing with sound doctrine when he exclaims, "We sometimes have intimations clear of wider scope, hints of occasions infinite."

The validity of the intimations of immortality is attested by the notable people who have felt them. The finest minds and most sensitive souls among us have followed this instinct of immortality with a child-like faith. John Morley waves a gallant farewell as he concludes his *Book of Recollections,* saying, "So to my home and in the falling twilight." To what home did he refer? Surely, no other than that promised by Jesus—"I go to prepare a place for you."

Tennyson, one of the finest souls of our Anglo-Saxon heritage, calls out in faith—

> "Thou wilt not leave us in the dust,
>   Thou madest man, he knows not why;
>   He thinks he was not made to die.
> Thou hast made him; thou art just."

Stevenson, that joyous and eternally youthful spirit, despite his long battle with the medicine bottle, awaits the touch of death in his island in the Pacific with these brave words:

> "The breeze from the embalmed land
>   Blows sudden toward the shore
>   And claps my cottage door—
>   I hear the signal, Lord,
> I understand;
>   The night at thy command
>   Comes;
> I will eat and sleep,
>   And will not question more."

Even Robert Ingersoll gave expression to a heart-deep faith in immortality when, standing by the body of his dead brother, he said, "Life is a narrow vale

between the cold and barren peaks of two eternities.
We strive in vain to look beyond the heights; we cry
aloud and the only answer is the echo of our wailing
cry. From the voiceless lips of the unreplying dead
there comes no word; but in the night of death hope
sees a star and listening love can hear the rustle of a
wing."

Can these fine minds have been wrong? Is it possible
that they and countless other, though less famous, men
and women, have been deluded? Can the lofty intuitions of these sensitive spirits be false? Like Job, who
among us has not cried, "If a man die, shall he live
again?"

We have considered the arguments for and against,
have weighed the evidence and scanned the horizon of
the years and have been unsatisfied. Then at last in
the regions of faith, ringing clearly like the notes of a
silver bell, we have heard a voice vibrant with authority, the voice of Jesus, "If it were *not* so, I would have
told you." Thus we may believe that the deepest intuitions and profoundest faith of the human soul in its
moments of luminous insight will not betray us. The
intimation of immortality finds definite basis in two
great facts—what God is and what man is. It finds its
validity in the worth of man and the character of God.
What values are there in human life which give it the
hint of eternity? There is, first, the thrill of man to
beauty which stirs and woos him with an irresistible
lure. It makes him conscious of a beauty within.

He looks, for example, upon Mount Shasta on a clear
morning, when the great cone of the mountain towers
above the wooded hillsides of California, its ermine
mantle of snow gleaming like myriads of diamonds in
the sunlight, its waterfalls spurting like scintillating
jewels into great dizzy valleys, its murmuring rivers

wending their way to the sea. He sees and hears and is conscious of the vastness and cleanness of the world. It calls to a greatness and cleanness in his own heart. He stands by the brink of the Grand Canyon in the crisp air of the Arizona uplands and watches the brilliant colors of gold and red and scarlet merging into the eerie shadows until purple twilight softly covers the towers, domes, and minarets of the vast abyss. Standing in the midst of that mighty silence, where nature before his very eyes is carving her story upon the rocks, he feels so deeply that it awes him—a profound affinity between the age-old world and his own soul. He wanders through a woodland, listening to the myriad sounds of life, conscious of the healing touch of nature. He sits beneath a tree and watches the sunlight as its plashes down between the branches onto the dark earth beneath and, like Wordsworth at Tintern Abbey, feels not only a Presence that disturbs him with the joy of elevated thought, but also a something far more deeply interfused, which rolls through all things and comes to rest finally in his own soul.

Another value in man suggesting immortality is his response to the ideal—to goodness. Phillips Brooks once said a great thing—"We are haunted by the ideal life; it is in our blood and will never be still." Man may fail to follow the ideal life and may not yield to its impulses, but he cannot escape from its constant resurgence in his soul. It will forever lure him. Whence come these mystic impulses toward goodness? Surely from divinity deep within the breast, straining ever toward the pure heights of life. Because it is there and ever persists, may we not conclude that it is ultimate in any characterization we may make of human life?

Man's capacity for insight and intuition also bears

witness to his immortality. Intuition may be defined as that knowledge which is above reason. It is man's highest faculty and goes where reason cannot go. It is a quality earlier than the intellectual process and therefore more pre-emptory and decisive. The validity of the intuitions was recognized by the great thinker, Henri Bergson. "Some other faculty," he said, "than the intellect is necessary for the apprehension of reality." Emerson likewise supports the right of intuitions to our respect by saying, "When God wants to carry a point with his children, he plants his argument in the instincts."

Once, twice, perhaps three times in a life, under some stress or sorrow, straining our ears we hear a reassuring voice, and shading our eyes we see intimations of an immortality to be. The Christian heart believes that if these intuitions and instincts were not so, he would have told us. We rest our faith in immortality upon the reliability of Jesus. He knew our longings and understood our intuitions. Had there been no objective reality in the direction in which they point, he would have told us. On the contrary, while he did not explain the afterlife, he gave us sublime hope by telling us our intuitions are trustworthy—"If it were *not so,* I would have told you."

The second great intimation of immortality is found in the character of God. We believe the soul was not made to be destroyed but will live on because of what God apparently is. We believe he is intelligent, and everywhere in the universe are evidences in support of that belief. The mark of intelligence is law and order and perfect precision. Here is a great skyscraper towering fifty, sixty, seventy stories above the street. It is built to the fraction of an inch on law. Would we not be very foolish to say that this great universe, infi-

nitely more intricate and complicated than any man-
made structure, came into being without personal intelligence? Moreover, any person of intelligence will
recognize an article of intrinsic worth and become a
conservator of values. If a person is wasteful or destructive or even careless, his intellectual capacity is
called into question. Thus we sometimes speak con-
temptuously of a fool and his money as being soon
parted.

Observe the values God has created. He has made
men like Shakespeare, Milton, Aristotle, Socrates, Lincoln, and a host of others less known but whose personalities have been radiant and whose efforts have been
creative. Would it be the mark of intelligence to permit the destruction of such marvelous creation at the
end of three-score years and ten? Would God do what
any intelligent individual would not do? The mere
thought is inconceivable. No, Emerson is right—"What
is excellent, as God lives, is permanent"—in a house, in
a world, or in a life.

We regard God as a Father, loving and just. That is
what Jesus said he is, and because of Jesus, with his
goodness and sacrificial spirit, his beauty of life, we
believe that God is like that. Could a father thrust his
children away? But one may raise the question—behold the pain and sorrow in the world. Would God,
as a Father, permit his children to suffer in this
manner? I think of my own father. He loves me; he
would give his life for me; he has sacrificed many things
for me, but I remember a room where my father and I
used to retire on occasion, where he practiced the lay-
ing on of hands in an unecclesiastical manner, finish-
ing with that ancient parental excuse, that it hurt him
more than it did me. I needed such parental disci-
pline, else I would grow to manhood soft and with only

a partial appreciation of life's disciplinary values. But I remember other times, many of them, when my father in love and tenderness put his hand upon my head or his arms of protection about me.

Thus, when one becomes a man, he is but a child grown larger, and when the Great Father of the universe disciplines him, surely he will not conclude that love does not exist. The assured love of God leads us back finally to that great text with which we may reassure ourselves regarding personal immortality—"If it were *not* so, I would have told you."

So I am asking you to follow no intricate and reasoned argument but to have faith—a faith like that of a little child who believes that nothing is too good to be true. Whittier gave expression to this faith.

> "O love will dream and faith will trust,
> Since he who knows our need is just,
> That somehow, somewhere, meet we must.
> Alas for him who never sees
> The stars shine through his cypress trees,
> Who hopeless lays his dead away,
> Nor looks to see the breaking day
> Across the mournful marbles play;
> Who hath not learned in hours of faith
> This truth, to sense and flesh unknown—
> That life is ever Lord of Death,
> And love can never lose its own."

Remember those words from the Bible—"If it were *not* so, I would have told you." That is to say, trust that instinct in your heart which tells you that somewhere, somehow, you will meet your loved ones again in a land that is fairer than day, where there is neither sorrow nor suffering, where "God shall wipe away all tears from their eyes."

15743